Bedford/St. Martin's,
the premier publisher of composition readers,
is pleased to introduce:

THE ST. MARTIN'S CUSTOM READER

Edited by

LYNN Z. BLOOM
University of Connecticut
LOUISE Z. SMITH
University of Massachusetts, Boston

The only reader in America based on empirical research into what composition teachers actually use in their classrooms and what works best.

WHAT YOU'LL FIND IN THIS BOOKLET

IN KEEPING WITH THE QUALITY THAT HAS ALWAYS DISTINGUISHED BEDFORD/ST. MARTIN'S PUBLICATIONS, *THE ST. MARTIN'S CUSTOM READER* OFFERS THESE OUTSTANDING FEATURES

✔ The only reader based on research into what is actually taught in freshman composition.

The St. Martin's Custom Reader grows directly out of Lynn Z. Bloom's "Essay Canon" research, which identified not only the essays that have been taught most often but also the qualities of those essays that account for their teachability. Beginning with the original research, which surveyed the content of every composition reader published in four or more editions between 1946 and 1996, Professor Bloom expanded that research through the present day so that *The St. Martin's Custom Reader* database includes not only classic classroom favorites but also essays by up-and-coming writers whose works have approached canonical status in the past five years.

✔ Authors and essays that instructors want to teach and students want to read.

Reflecting the interests and needs of today's instructors and students, the database of *The St. Martin's Custom Reader* offers approximately 240 thoroughly class-tested essays that are the best available reading selections for first-year writing students. To ensure that instructors have abundant choices, 12 outstanding and often-anthologized authors—Judith Ortiz Cofer, Joan Didion, Annie Dillard, Henry Louis Gates Jr., Stephen Jay Gould, George Orwell, Gary Soto, Shelby Steele, Amy Tan, Deborah Tannen, Lewis Thomas, and Henry David Thoreau—are represented by three or more selections.

✔ **Carefully crafted headnotes enhance the reading experience.**

The unusually extensive headnotes in *The St. Martin's Custom Reader* provide thorough biographical, historical, and cultural information about each author and selection. In addition, the headnotes include commentary, often by the authors themselves or by contemporary writers and critics, that sheds light on the authors' work.

✔ **A book that is as easy to create as it is to use.**

Instructors can create their custom readers online at the Bedford/St. Martin's Web site, at http://customreader.bedfordstmartins.com. The contents of this booklet mirror the Web site, offering all the information instructors need to build a custom reader, including an annotated table of contents of all the essays in the database, with a brief description of each, as well as alternative arrangements of the essays by rhetorical strategies and by themes. A separate CD-ROM, included at the back of this booklet, will enable instructors to preview the full text of the selections in the custom reader database before making their choices. (The CD-ROM is *not required* for building a custom reader online—only for previewing selections.) Instructors who prefer to place their custom reader requests by fax may do so by printing a hard copy of our order form from the corresponding link on the CD-ROM and faxing it to our custom publishing department.

ABOUT THE EDITORS

Lynn Z. Bloom is Board of Trustees Distinguished Professor and holder of the Aetna Chair of Writing at the University of Connecticut. Previously, she taught and directed writing programs at Butler University, the University of New Mexico, and the College of William and Mary, and she chaired the English department at Virginia Commonwealth University. Lynn Bloom's publications include composition studies, biography, autobiography, creative nonfiction, poetry, reviews, articles, book chapters, and textbooks. *The Essay Canon*, a book-length version of her 1999 journal article, will be published by the University of Wisconsin Press in 2003.

Louise Z. Smith is Professor of English and chair of the English department at the University of Massachusetts, Boston. A member of the faculty there since 1974, she also served as the Director of Freshman English, Director of the Tutoring Program, and Director, Core Curriculum. In addition to the many articles and book chapters she has written for publication, Louise Smith was the editor of *College English* from 1991 to 1999, and she remains a member of its editorial advisory board.

LYNN Z. BLOOM ON "THE ESSAY CANON" RESEARCH AND *THE ST. MARTIN'S CUSTOM READER*

The St. Martin's Custom Reader is the only reader in America compiled entirely of essays by writers whose works have a history of repeated classroom use. Each essayist is a contributor to the essay canon—one of the nearly 200 writers whose essays are the most widely reprinted in college textbooks. The list of these writers is derived from my five years of research on "The Essay Canon" (*College English*, March 1999, 401–30). Thus *The St. Martin's Custom Reader* is the only college textbook in the United States whose contents are totally based on empirical research into what composition teachers actually use in their classrooms, and what works best.

The essay canon—as represented in my research and translated into the list of essays included in *The St. Martin's Custom Reader*—is a *teaching* canon as distinct from a *critical* canon. It is unique in this respect, for although other literary canons—of works by novelists, poets, playwrights—are determined by the esteem of editors, reviewers, and critics, the essay canon is the only canon determined by teachers and, indirectly, by their students. Not only is it the most democratic canon, but it is the canon with the most real-world orientation. The works in this canon may, indeed, constitute the core of a liberal education for many first-year college students.

The Research Question

Seven years ago I casually asked the questions that would subsequently change my life. "What essays do people read today?" I wondered. "And where do they read them?" The short answer is, "Those Americans who read essays at all find them reprinted in composition readers, anthologies intended for first-year writing courses." No matter where an essay first appeared—whether in *The New Yorker* or in another magazine or on a newspaper's op-ed page—if it is to survive in the hearts and minds of the reading public, it must be reprinted time after time in a textbook reader. Only if it appears repeatedly in readers does it stand the chance of reaching—and influencing—a significant number of America's 2.5 million first-year college students.

The Research Method

I quickly rejected the easy solution—to look around my study and see what essays were printed in the books I had on hand. And I just as quickly decided to focus on the most influential readers, reasoning that the most widely read essays would appear repeatedly in the most widely adopted collections. I defined these as books published in four or more editions over a 50-year span, from the end of World War II to the present—58 titles published in 325 volumes.

It took five years to locate all the books, to compile a database of their complete tables of contents, and to check and recheck the numbers. This compresses into a 64-page alphabetical listing of all the 4,246 writers whose works are included in the canonical textbooks—some 21,000 reprintings of some 8,000 different essay titles. Any writer whose works were reprinted 20 or more times during the past 50 years was considered canonical. There were 175 writers whose works constituted nearly half of the total reprints.

The Canonical Essayists

The canonical essayists included 18 superstars whose works were reprinted 100 or more times, among them George Orwell, E. B. White, Joan Didion, Lewis Thomas, H. D. Thoreau, Virginia Woolf, Jonathan Swift, and Martin Luther King Jr. There were 15 stars, whose works were reprinted 70 to 99 times, ranging from Richard Rodriguez, Plato, and Alice Walker, to Isaac Asimov, H. L. Mencken, and Judy [Syfers] Brady, author of "I Want a Wife." Among the remaining 142 luminaries are Jessica Mitford, Francis Bacon, N. Scott Momaday, Maxine Hong Kingston, and Gloria Steinem, among others.

The works of all of these canonical essayists are included in *The St. Martin's Custom Reader*, with two types of exceptions. There were a few writers for whom we unfortunately could not obtain reprint permissions, including Woody Allen, Robert Coles, Jamaica Kincaid, Adrienne Rich, and Studs Terkel. In addition, because literary canons are alive and continually growing and changing, Louise Z. Smith, coeditor of *The St. Martin's Custom Reader*, and I decided to omit around 30 writers whose works were not reprinted during the past decade in order to make room for up-and-coming writers whose works have approached canonical status in the past five years, since the original research was completed in 1996. Thus we have updated the canon—and the table of contents here—to include such rising stars as Diane Ackerman, Dave Barry, John Berger, Judith Ortiz Cofer, Henry Louis Gates Jr., Barbara Kingsolver, Mike Rose, Gary Soto, Amy Tan, Patricia Williams, and Terry Tempest Williams.

About 60 percent of the canonical essayists are professional writers—journalists, belletristic essayists, novelists, satirists, poets, critics. Most of the others are distinguished scholars or other professionals in varied fields whose writing is clear and accessible to a general readership—scientists, educators, theologians, psychologists, linguists, historians, and so on.

The Canonical Essays

To become a candidate for canonicity, and for *The St. Martin's Custom Reader*, an essay must first and foremost be teachable; it must contribute to the intellectual, political, and rhetorical balance of the whole book; and it must be very well written. Whether and how an essay will work in the classroom is an overriding concern.

- An essay's teachability is determined in part by its level of difficulty. How much do teachers have to know or learn in order to teach the work? Will students understand its concepts and vocabulary, with or without much explanation in class? Is it intellectually appropriate for them? Is it too technical, too allusive, too arty for students to stick with it? Length, too, is important; is the essay short enough to be discussed in one or two class periods?
- An essay's balance with the rest of the book is reflected in the ways that its topic, point of view, and moral and ethical stance contribute to the kinds of dialogue, debate, and critical thinking the anthology hopes to engender. Will it enlarge the students' understanding of the world, or of a particular issue? Does the essay represent views and values that students should consider, confront, and either challenge or adopt? Does the writer's reputation, their ethnicity, gender, or stand on issues contribute to the anthology's balanced perspective?
- An essay's aesthetic qualities are related to form. Is the essay a good rhetorical model, for example, of description or comparison and contrast? Does it exemplify notable rhetorical techniques of, say, definition, narration, or argument? The writer's technique is important, too. Is the essay technically interesting and sufficiently well written to serve as a good model for organization, style, vocabulary, tone, even wit? Does the writer "make it new," enabling readers to see the subject afresh?

Finally, for an essay to swim from the vast pool of essays being published every year to a wider range of readers, and from there to ascend to the list of canonical essays that comprise *The St. Martin's Custom Reader*, teachers around the country have had to like (if not love) the essay, find it exciting, and expect that their students will benefit from reading it. An advantage of this custom reader is that all teachers selecting from its contents can include in their own compilations exactly those essays best suited to their own teaching and their own students, confident that their choices have already been tested in classrooms throughout the country.

THE ANNOTATED TABLE OF CONTENTS FOR *THE ST. MARTIN'S CUSTOM READER*

EDWARD ABBEY, ***The Serpents of Paradise*** *(6 pp.)*

Abbey, a pioneer of radical environmental activism, writes lyrically of the Southwestern landscape and angrily about the tourists, corporations, and governmental agencies that threaten it. Here he cautions—or boasts—"I prefer not to kill animals. I'm a humanist; I'd rather kill a *man* than a snake."

Strategies: Description, Narration

Themes: Ethics/Values, Nature, Environment, Places

DIANE ACKERMAN, ***Why Leaves Turn Color in the Fall*** *(4 pp.)*

Ackerman, poet and naturalist, explains natural phenomena in graceful language underpinned by scientific knowledge. Here she promotes our understanding of science and celebrates the natural world: "When the days begin to shorten, soon after the summer solstice on June 21, a tree reconsiders its leaves."

Strategies: Description, Process Analysis

Themes: Science, Nature

MAYA ANGELOU, ***Champion of the World*** *(4 pp.)*

Recalling her childhood in the 1930s, poet and memoirist Angelou describes listening to the radio in her family's general store, as Joe Louis defended his heavyweight championship title against a white contender: "Champion of the world. A Black boy. Some Black mother's son . . . the strongest man in the world."

Strategies: Narration, Analogy

Themes: Human/Civil Rights, Family, Places, Community

MAYA ANGELOU, ***Graduation*** *(11 pp.)*

Poet and memoirist Angelou recalls anticipating her eighth-grade graduation ceremony in rural Arkansas. When at the ceremony a condescending white speaker consigns the black graduates to little more than menial jobs, the class valedictorian restores the graduates' dignity: "I was a proud member of the wonderful, beautiful Negro race."

Strategies: Compare/Contrast, Description, Narration

Themes: Human/Civil Rights, Family, Places, Coming of Age, Community

GLORIA ANZALDÚA, ***How to Tame a Wild Tongue (12 pp.)***

Anzaldúa, who identifies herself as feminist, lesbian, Chicana, and *mestiza* (a person of mixed Indian and Spanish ancestry), explores the struggle to define an identity. She insists that "I will no longer be made to feel ashamed of existing. I will have my voice: Indian, Spanish, white. I will have my serpent's tongue—my woman's voice, my sexual voice, my poet's voice."

Strategies: Narration, Metaphor, Argument and Persuasion

Themes: Cultural Diversity, Places, Community, Gender, Language

ISAAC ASIMOV, ***The Eureka Phenomenon (11 pp.)***

Asimov, scientist and prolific writer, explains the role of involuntary reasoning in the creative process: "Suddenly I would find I had written myself into a hole and could see no way out. To take care of that, I developed a technique which invariably worked. It was simply this—I went to the movies."

Strategies: Definition, Illustration, Process Analysis

Theme: Science, Writing, Work (and Play)

MARGARET ATWOOD, ***The Page (2 pp.)***

In response to the question "Why do you write?" Canadian novelist Atwood offers a series of oblique images that represent the blank page as a writer sees it: a directionless and dimensionless terrain where "you can become lost . . . forever."

Strategies: Analogy, Metaphor, Process Analysis

Theme: Writing

MARGARET ATWOOD, ***Pornography (6 pp.)***

Novelist Atwood expresses her concerns about the potential harm of violent pornography and the prospect that erotica of all sorts could be banned. In answer to the question "what's the harm?" she replies, "Nobody knows, but this society should find out fast, before the saturation point is reached."

Strategies: Definition, Illustration, Argument and Persuasion

Themes: Ethics/Values, Human/Civil Rights, Gender

FRANCIS BACON, ***The Four Idols** (9 pp.)*

Bacon, one of the greatest thinkers of the English Renaissance, identifies four "idols," or illusions, that interfere with true understanding of the world around us.

Strategies: Definition, Classification/Division, Argument and Persuasion
Themes: Ethics/Values, Science

RUSSELL BAKER, ***The Plot Against People** (3 pp.)*

Baker, longtime *New York Times* columnist, wittily satirizes the annoyances of ordinary life: "Inanimate objects are classified scientifically into three major categories—those that don't work, those that break down, and those that get lost."

Strategies: Classification/Division, Satire
Theme: Popular Culture

JAMES BALDWIN, ***Notes of a Native Son** (18 pp.)*

Novelist and essayist Baldwin writes about the death of his deeply embittered stepfather, an event that coincided with a violent race riot in Harlem in 1943. Driving through the wreckage on the way to the cemetery, he notes, "I hated the unbelievable streets and the Negroes and whites who had, equally, made them that way."

Strategies: Illustration, Narration
Themes: Human/Civil Rights, Cultural Diversity, Family, Coming of Age

JAMES BALDWIN, ***Stranger in the Village** (9 pp.)*

In this excerpt from *Notes of a Native Son*, Baldwin tells the story of his experience as the only black person living in a Swiss village, where he reaches a deeper understanding of "the battle waged by [white] Americans to maintain between themselves and black men a human separation which could not be bridged."

Strategies: Narration, Argument and Persuasion
Themes: Human/Civil Rights, Cultural Diversity, Places, Language

DAVE BARRY, ***In Depth, But Shallowly** (4 pp.)*

Humorist Barry prompts a critical reading of local TV newscasts with their stereotypical role assignments and their superficial coverage of issues: "And now, as I promised earlier, we have actual color film of various objects that either burned or crashed, which we will project on the screen behind me while I talk about them."

Strategies: Illustration, Satire
Theme: Popular Culture

WILLIAM J. BENNETT, ***What Really Ails America*** *(5 pp.)*

Bennett, a conservative commentator, contends that America faces a spiritual crisis. To save our nation, he asserts, "we must return religion to its proper place. . . . The surrendering of strong beliefs, in our private and public lives, has demoralized society."

Strategies: Comparison/Contrast, Illustration, Argument and Persuasion
Themes: Ethics/Values, Politics/Government, Family

JOHN BERGER, ***Ways of Seeing*** *(24 pp.)*

Berger, best known for his Marxist art criticism, focuses on the processes of seeing and the cultural dimensions of art. Rejecting abstract notions of "beauty," Berger believes that "the real question is: To whom does the meaning of the art of the past properly belong? to those who can apply it to their own lives, or to a cultural hierarchy of relic specialists?"

Strategies: Illustration, Argument and Persuasion
Themes: Ethics/Values

WENDELL BERRY, ***Home of the Free*** *(4 pp.)*

A writer, environmentalist, and farmer, Berry decries our tendency to allow technology to insulate us from reality: "We do not want to experience temperatures that are the least bit too hot or too cold, or to work in the sun, or be exposed to wind or rain, or come in personal contact with anything describable as dirt, or provide for any of our own needs, or clean up after ourselves."

Strategies: Illustration, Argument and Persuasion
Themes: Environment, Popular Culture

BRUNO BETTELHEIM, ***Joey: A "Mechanical Boy"*** *(9 pp.)*

Psychologist Bettelheim offers this case study of an autistic child and his recovery as a parable for our times: "When the individual has escaped into a delusional world, he has usually fashioned it from bits and pieces of the world at hand. . . . [Joey's] story has a general relevance to the understanding of emotional development in a machine age."

Strategies: Illustration, Cause/Effect
Themes: Science, Family

CAROL BLY, ***Getting Tired*** **(5 *pp.*)**

Bly, an essayist and short-story writer who often focuses on rural life, recounts her experience running a plow as a farm day-laborer and reflects on the psychological effects of such work: "A thousand impressions enter as you work up and down the rows: nature's beauty or nature's stubbornness, politics, exhaustion, but mainly the feeling that all this repetition . . . is taking up your lifetime."

Strategies: Narration, Cause/Effect
Themes: Environment, Work (and Play)

WAYNE BOOTH, ***Boring from Within: The Art of the Freshman Essay*** **(10 *pp.*)**

Booth, a critic and English teacher, looks at the problems with student writing in typical freshman composition classes: "Our students bore us, even when they take a seemingly lively controversial tone, because they have nothing to say, to us or to anybody else. If and when they discover something to say, they will no longer bore us, and our comments will no longer bore them."

Strategies: Classification/Division, Process Analysis
Themes: Writing, Education

JUDY BRADY, ***I Want a Wife*** **(4 *pp.*)**

Brady's 1970 essay on the advantages of having a wife—defined as a partner who devotes her life to pleasing her spouse with no expectation of reciprocity—concludes with the declaration, "My God, who *wouldn't* want a wife?"

Strategies: Comparison/Contrast, Definition, Classification/Division
Themes: Human/Civil Rights, Gender

SUZANNE BRITT, ***That Lean and Hungry Look*** **(4 *pp.*)**

Britt, writer and self-described plump person, plays off the stereotypes of fat people and thin people, arguing tongue-in-cheek that fat people are better in every way: "In the first place, thin people aren't fun. They don't know how to goof off, at least in the best, fat sense of the word."

Strategies: Comparison/Contrast, Classification/Division
Themes: Ethics/Values, Popular Culture

JANE BRODY, ***Exercise: A New Dietary Requirement*** **(10 *pp.*)**

Brody, the *New York Times* "Personal Health" columnist, extols the benefits of regular exercise: "I, along with millions of Americans, have discovered that exercise is the key to permanent and painless weight control."

Strategies: Definition, Process Analysis
Themes: Science, Work (and Play)

JACOB BRONOWSKI, ***The Reach of Imagination*** *(7 pp.)*

Bronowski, a twentieth-century scientist and mathematician, suggests that "imagination is a specifically *human* gift" available not only to poets and scientists but to us all: "Almost everything that we do that is worth doing is done in the first place in the mind's eye."

Strategies: Definition, Analogy, Metaphor
Themes: Science, Nature

WILLIAM F. BUCKLEY JR., ***Why Don't We Complain?*** *(6 pp.)*

Buckley, magazine editor and conservative columnist, explores the average American's reluctance to speak out about avoidable annoyances and relates this to the larger political arena: "When our voices are finally mute, when we have finally suppressed the natural instinct to complain, whether the vexation is trivial or grave, we shall have become automatons, incapable of feeling."

Strategies: Illustration, Narration, Cause/Effect
Themes: Ethics/Values, Popular Culture

RACHEL CARSON, ***Fable for Tomorrow*** *(2 pp.)*

In this opening chapter of *Silent Spring*, biologist and conservationist Carson envisions a future in which the cumulative effects of chemical pollution have devastated the environment. She warns that "no witchcraft, no enemy action had silenced the rebirth of new life in this stricken world. The people had done it themselves."

Strategies: Description, Illustration
Themes: Nature, Environment

STEPHEN CARTER, ***The Insufficiency of Honesty*** *(6 pp.)*

Carter, Yale Law School professor, examines the differences between *honesty* and, for him, the far greater virtue of *integrity*, which he describes as requiring three steps: "discerning what is right and what is wrong; acting on what you have discerned, even at personal cost; and saying openly that you are acting on your understanding of right and wrong."

Strategies: Comparison/Contrast, Definition, Illustration
Themes: Ethics/Values, Human/Civil Rights

BRUCE CATTON, ***Grant and Lee: A Study in Contrasts*** ***(4 pp.)***

A prolific historian of the American Civil War, Catton presents the leaders of the opposing Northern and Southern forces as embodiments of the cultures for which each fought: "They were strong men, these oddly different generals, and they represented the strengths of two conflicting currents that, through them, had come into final collision."

Strategies: Comparison/Contrast, Definition

Themes: Ethics/Values, Cultural Diversity

CURTIS CHANG, ***Streets of Gold: The Myth of the Model Minority*** ***(10 pp.)***

A Chinese immigrant, Chang wrote this essay when he was a freshman at Harvard University. He argues that portraying Asian Americans as exemplars of successful minorities in the United States "distorts Asian Americans' true status and ignores [their] racial handicaps. . . . It attempts to justify the existing system of racial inequality by blaming the victims rather than the system itself."

Strategies: Comparison/Contrast, Illustration, Argument and Persuasion

Themes: Ethics/Values, Cultural Diversity, Family, Work (and Play), Education

STEPHEN CHAPMAN, ***The Prisoner's Dilemma*** ***(8 pp.)***

Chapman, a journalist and libertarian, challenges his readers to rethink the assumption that Western culture is the most humane, finding that "at least in regard to cruelty, it's not at all clear that the system of punishment that has evolved in the West is less barbaric than the grotesque practices of Islam."

Strategies: Comparison/Contrast, Argument and Persuasion

Themes: Politics/Government, Human/Civil Rights

JOHN CIARDI, ***Is Everybody Happy?*** ***(4 pp.)***

Ciardi, poet and *Saturday Review* editor, rejects both the consumer culture and Eastern notions of happiness: "Whatever else happiness may be, it is neither in having nor in being, but in becoming."

Strategies: Comparison/Contrast, Definition

Themes: Ethics/Values, Popular Culture, Work (and Play)

SANDRA CISNEROS, ***Only Daughter*** ***(4 pp.)***

Cisneros, a poet and fiction writer, reflects on what it was like to grow up as the only daughter in a Mexican American family of six sons. Moreover, she explores her role in her culture as "*only* a daughter," which "for [her] father meant [her]

destiny would lead [her] to become someone's wife" rather than to have a career of her own.

Strategies: Comparison/Contrast, Definition, Narration
Themes: Cultural Diversity, Family, Work (and Play), Gender

JUDITH ORTIZ COFER, Casa: *A Partial Remembrance of a Puerto Rican Childhood (5 pp.)*

Cofer, an essayist and poet, recalls her grandmother passing on *cuentos*, cautionary tales designed to save women from male perfidy and their own gullibility. On the brink of adolescence, she listened intently to these tales, "trying to fit it all together like a puzzle that, once assembled, would reveal life's mysteries."

Strategy: Narration
Themes: Cultural Diversity, Family, Gender, Language

JUDITH ORTIZ COFER, *More Room (4 pp.)*

Cofer offers the many rooms of her Puerto Rican grandmother's house as a metaphor for her grandmother's life. After giving birth to eleven children—and having her husband add rooms accordingly—she has him add a room of his own as a way of asserting "the right to own and control her body . . . so that she could give more of herself to the ones already there, so that she could be more than a channel for other lives."

Strategies: Description, Narration, Metaphor
Themes: Family, Gender

JUDITH ORTIZ COFER, *The Myth of the Latin Woman (5 pp.)*

Cofer draws on personal experience to describe the kinds of cultural stereotyping that Latin women too often encounter, particularly "the Hispanic woman as the 'hot tamale' or sexual firebrand" and that of "the menial, the domestic—Maria the housemaid or countergirl."

Strategies: Illustration, Narration
Themes: Human/Civil Rights, Cultural Diversity, Family, Gender

K. C. COLE, *Women in Science (4 pp.)*

Cole, a science writer, argues that formidable social barriers discourage women who are interested in science and math from pursuing their interests. Women in these fields, she states, are made to "feel unnecessary, and out of place."

Strategies: Illustration, Narration, Argument and Persuasion
Themes: Human/Civil Rights, Science, Gender

STEPHANIE COONTZ, ***A Nation of Welfare Families*** *(5 pp.)*

Coontz, an academic and family historian, argues that since the founding of our country, American families in every income bracket—not just the poor—"have depended on the legislative, judicial, and social support structures" to attain educational and financial success.

Strategies: Comparison/Contrast, Illustration, Argument and Persuasion
Themes: Ethics/Values, Politics/Government, Family, Work (and Play)

AARON COPLAND, ***How We Listen to Music*** *(6 pp.)*

Copland, influential modern American composer, urges listeners to attend simultaneously to the sensory, expressive, and formal qualities of music, becoming "not someone who is just listening, but someone who is listening *for* something."

Strategies: Definition, Classification/Division, Description
Theme: Popular Culture

NORMAN COUSINS, ***Pain Is Not the Ultimate Enemy*** *(4 pp.)*

Cousins, a *Saturday Review* editor, used his own life-threatening illnesses as the basis for his explorations of the psychological dimensions of disease. Here he asserts that "nothing is more remarkable about the human body than its recuperative drive, given a modicum of respect."

Strategies: Argument and Persuasion
Themes: Science, Popular Culture

CHARLES DARWIN, ***Understanding Natural Selection*** *(5 pp.)*

Naturalist Darwin discovered the mechanism of natural selection, which underlies the theory of evolution and explains how species make the gradual adaptations that enable their survival: "in a state of nature, where the trees would have to struggle with other trees and with a host of enemies, such differences would effectually settle which variety, whether a smooth or downy, a yellow or purple fleshed fruit, should succeed."

Strategies: Comparison/Contrast, Definition, Cause/Effect
Themes: Science, Environment

JOAN DIDION, ***Marrying Absurd*** *(4 pp.)*

In this 1967 essay, Didion illustrates the ironic disjunction between the traditional rituals of marriage and the gaudy, twenty-four-hour-a-day wedding business in Las Vegas, where chapels compete to merchandise "'niceness,' the facsimile of proper ritual, to children who do not know how else to find it, how to make the arrangements, how to do it 'right.'"

Strategies: Definition, Classification/Division, Analogy, Metaphor

Themes: Ethics/Values, Family, Popular Culture, Places

JOAN DIDION, ***On Going Home*** **(3 pp.)**

During a stay with her parents in the house where she grew up, Didion reflects on "the neurotic lassitude engendered by meeting one's past at every turn" and wonders whether the same attachment to home exists for later generations.

Strategies: Comparison/Contrast, Definition, Description

Themes: Ethics/Values, Family, Places

JOAN DIDION, ***On Keeping a Notebook*** **(7 pp.)**

In this essay, Didion reflects on her "impulse to write things down," to record her observations of those around her: "I imagine . . . that the notebook is about other people. But of course it is not. . . . *Remember what it was to be me:* that is always the point."

Strategies: Definition, Illustration

Themes: Writing, Coming of Age

JOAN DIDION, ***Some Dreamers of the Golden Dream*** **(13 pp.)**

Didion uses a true story of adultery, murder, and betrayal to illustrate the unrootedness of California in the 1960s: "Here is the last stop for all those who come from somewhere else, for all those who drifted away from the cold and the past and the old ways."

Strategies: Definition, Description, Narration

Themes: Ethics/Values, Family, Popular Culture

ANNIE DILLARD, ***Death of a Moth*** **(4 pp.)**

A keen and lyrical observer of the natural world, Dillard here finds a metaphor for the artistic impulse in the image of a moth trapped in a candle flame: "She burned for two hours without changing . . . only glowing within, like a building fire glimpsed through silhouetted walls, like a hollow saint, like a flame-faced virgin gone to God, while I read by her light."

Strategies: Description, Narration, Analogy, Metaphor

Themes: Nature, Writing

ANNIE DILLARD, ***Seeing*** **(12 pp.)**

In this essay, Dillard explores with pleasure and awe the universe as it is revealed through the act of seeing, from observing the heavens to peering into the smallest forms of life: "Often I slop some creek water in a jar. . . . After the silt settles I return and see tracings of minute snails on the bottom, a planarian or two winding round the rim of water, roundworms shimmying, frantically, and finally, when my eyes have adjusted to these dimensions, amoebae."

Strategies: Comparison/Contrast, Description, Illustration
Themes: Ethics/Values, Science, Nature

ANNIE DILLARD, ***The Stunt Pilot*** ***(10 pp.)***

In an expert stunt pilot's magnificent loops and arabesques, Dillard sees close parallels to the work of the creative artist: "[H]e fulfilled your hope slantingly, like a poet, or evaded it until you thought you would burst, and then fulfilled it surprisingly, so you gasped and cried out."

Strategies: Description, Narration, Analogy, Metaphor
Themes: Ethics/Values, Writing, Work (and Play)

JOHN DONNE, ***No Man Is an Island*** ***(2 pp.)***

The seventeenth century metaphysical poet and preacher John Donne, in this often quoted meditation, highlights our common fate and our interconnectedness: "No man is an island, entire of itself; every man is a piece of the continent, a part of the main."

Strategies: Analogy, Metaphor
Themes: Ethics/Values, Human/Civil Rights

MICHAEL DORRIS, ***For Indians, No Thanksgiving*** ***(3 pp.)***

Dorris, a Native American writer and student of Native American culture, contrasts "Hollywood Indians"—crowd-pleasing, "manageable, domesticated inventions" of their white conquerors—with today's reservation Indians: "the ethnic group at the wrong extreme of every scale: most undernourished, most short-lived, least educated, least healthy."

Strategies: Comparison/Contrast, Illustration
Themes: Ethics/Values, Politics/Government, Human/Civil Rights

FREDERICK DOUGLASS, ***Resurrection*** ***(5 pp.)***

Abolitionist Frederick Douglass narrates a critical "turning-point" in his life: "You have seen how a man was made a slave; you shall see how a slave was made a man."

Strategies: Definition, Narration, Analogy
Themes: Ethics/Values, Politics/Government, Human/Civil Rights

ESTHER DYSON, *Cyberspace for All* *(5 pp.)*

Dyson, a visionary information technologist, argues against governmental regulation of the Internet: "We haven't created a perfect society on earth and we won't have one in cyberspace either. But at least we can have individual choice—and individual responsibility."

Strategies: Comparison/Contrast, Illustration, Argument and Persuasion
Themes: Ethics/Values, Politics/Government, Human/Civil Rights, Science

BARBARA EHRENREICH, *Oh,* Those *Family Values* *(3 pp.)*

Journalist Ehrenreich, a feminist and socialist, argues that, in contradiction to our myth that families are "the ideal unit of human community," many families are "a nest of pathology and a cradle of gruesome violence."

Strategies: Comparison/Contrast, Definition, Argument and Persuasion
Themes: Ethics/Values, Family, Popular Culture

GRETEL EHRLICH, *The Solace of Open Spaces* *(10 pp.)*

For writer Gretel Ehrlich the "open country" and vital people of her new surroundings on the Wyoming plains bring about a psychic rebirth: "I threw away my clothes and bought new ones; I cut my hair. The arid country was a clean slate. Its absolute indifference steadied me."

Strategies: Definition, Narration, Cause/Effect
Themes: Ethics/Values, Nature, Places

LARS EIGHNER, *On Dumpster Diving* *(11 pp.)*

Writer Lars Eighner's essay on his experience as a homeless person is written in the present tense: "I live from the refuse of others. I am a scavenger. I think it a sound and honorable niche, although if I could I would naturally prefer to live the comfortable consumer life, perhaps—and only perhaps—as a slightly less wasteful consumer, owing to what I have learned as a scavenger."

Strategies: Definition, Classification/Division
Themes: Popular Culture, Work (and Play)

LOREN EISELEY, *The Brown Wasps* *(7 pp.)*

In a mixture of poetic language and precise science, anthropologist Eiseley presents several analogies to illustrate the long-term persistence of memory, even for things long gone: "We cling to a time and place because without them man is lost, not only man but life."

Strategies: Description, Narration, Analogy

Themes: Science, Nature, Environment

PETER ELBOW, ***Freewriting*** *(4 pp.)*

Composition innovator Elbow explains his popular technique of freewriting: "Make some words, whatever they are, and then grab hold of that line and reel in as hard as you can. Afterwards you can throw away lousy beginnings and make new ones. This is the quickest way to get into good writing."

Strategies: Definition, Illustration

Theme: Writing

RALPH ELLISON, ***On Being the Target of Discrimination*** *(7 pp.)*

Recounting the pain and absurdity of racial discrimination, writer Ellison remembers a childhood marked by segregation: "It was said by word of mouth, proclaimed in newsprint, and dramatized by acts of discriminatory law that you were inferior."

Strategy: Narration

Themes: Human/Civil Rights, Cultural Diversity, Coming of Age, Community

RALPH WALDO EMERSON, ***The American Scholar*** *(14 pp.)*

Emerson, a leader of the Transcendentalist movement in American literature, exhorts his audience to bring their own thoughts and experiences to their scholarship: "One must be an inventor to read well. . . . When the mind is braced by labor and invention, the page of whatever book we read becomes luminous with manifold allusion."

Strategies: Definition, Classification/Division, Argument and Persuasion

Theme: Education

NORA EPHRON, ***A Few Words about Breasts*** *(8 pp.)*

Ephron, a writer and film director, claims that "for most girls, breasts, brassieres, that entire thing, has more trauma, more to do with the coming of adolescence, with becoming a woman, than anything else."

Strategies: Illustration, Narration

Themes: Family, Coming of Age, Gender

JOSEPH EPSTEIN, ***The Virtues of Ambition*** *(5 pp.)*

Defending the ethic of individual choice and achievement, essayist Epstein laments that fact that "as drunks have done to alcohol, the single-minded have done to ambition—given it a bad name."

Strategy: Definition
Themes: Ethics/Values, Popular Culture, Community, Work (and Play)

LOUISE ERDRICH, ***Leap Day, the Baby-sitter, Dream, Walking*** *(5 pp.)*

In these sections from *The Blue Jay's Dance: A Birth Year*, Erdrich analyzes the complex process of being both a mother and a writer: "As our baby grows more into her own life, so I recover mine, but it is an ambiguous blessing. With one hand I drag the pen across the page and with the other, the other hand, I cannot let go of hers."

Strategies: Comparison/Contrast, Illustration, Narration
Themes: Ethics/Values, Cultural Diversity, Family, Work (and Play)

PETER FARB AND GEORGE ARMELAGOS, ***The Patterns of Eating*** *(5 pp.)*

Anthropologists Farb and Armelagos analyze the evolution of table manners from the Middle Ages to the present as a reflection of changes in relationships between humans and their food: "The present European pattern eventually emerged, in which each person is provided with a table setting of as many as a dozen utensils at a full-course meal. With that, the separation of the human body from the taking of food became virtually complete."

Strategies: Comparison/Contrast, Description
Themes: Ethics/Values, Science, Community

WILLIAM FAULKNER, ***Nobel Prize Award Speech*** *(2 pp.)*

In the aftermath of World War II and its spark of the nuclear age, novelist Faulkner urges younger writers to renew their optimism and to subscribe to his faith in the future: "I believe that man will not merely endure: he will prevail."

Strategies: Argument and Persuasion
Themes: Ethics/Values, Writing

ROBERT FINCH, ***Very Like a Whale*** *(5 pp.)*

Cape Cod nature writer Finch asserts that humans need to establish ways of relating to animals, ways that are neither exploitative nor sentimental: "Whales have an inalienable right to exist, not because they resemble man *or* because they are useful to him, but simply because they do exist."

Strategies: Description, Narration, Argument and Persuasion
Themes: Nature, Environment, Places

FRANCES FITZGERALD, ***Rewriting American History*** *(7 pp.)*

Tracing the changes in American history textbooks from the 1950s vision of a "perfect" America to the contemporary focus on social issues and problems, journalist FitzGerald makes the point that interpretations of history change dramatically as society changes: "The society that was once uniform is now a patchwork of rich and poor, old and young, men and women, blacks, whites, Hispanics, and Indians."

Strategy: Illustration

Themes: Politicians/Government, Cultural Diversity, Education

E. M. FORSTER, ***What I Believe*** *(8 pp.)*

Novelist Forster, writing at a time of great international upheaval, explores what he values in the human character: "I believe in aristocracy . . . Not an aristocracy of power, based upon rank and influence, but an aristocracy of the sensitive, the considerate, and the plucky. Its members are to be found in all nations and classes, and all through the ages."

Strategies: Comparison/Contrast, Definition, Argument and Persuasion

Themes: Ethics/Values, Politics/Government, Community

BENJAMIN FRANKLIN, ***Advice to a Young Tradesman, Written by an Old One. To My Friend A. B.*** *(3 pp.)*

Franklin, an American patriot and Renaissance man, offers advice for material success: "In short, the Way to Wealth, if you desire it, is as plain as the Way to Market. It depends chiefly on two Words, INDUSTRY and FRUGALITY; i.e., Waste neither Time nor Money, but make the best Use of both."

Strategies: Argument and Persuasion

Themes: Ethics/Values, Work (and Play)

SIGMUND FREUD, ***Libidinal Types*** *(4 pp.)*

Freud, the founder of psychoanalysis, identifies three distinctive personality types, defined in terms of their response to the instinctive sexual and creative drive: "We can distinguish three main libidinal types, according as the subject's libido is mainly allocated to one or another region of the mental apparatus. . . . I should be inclined to call them the *erotic*, the *narcissistic*, and the *obsessional* type."

Strategies: Definition, Classification/Division

Theme: Science

MILTON FRIEDMAN, ***Prohibition and Drugs*** *(3 pp.)*

Taking a controversial stand, economist Friedman argues against outlawing recreational drugs based on the analogy of legal prohibition of alcohol in the 1920s: "Prohibition undermined respect for the law, corrupted the minions of the law, created a decadent moral climate—but did not stop the consumption of alcohol. Despite this tragic object lesson, we seem bent on repeating precisely the same mistake in the handling of drugs."

Strategies: Illustration, Argument and Persuasion
Themes: Ethics/Values, Politics/Government

ERICH FROMM, ***The Theory of Love*** *(7 pp.)*

Psychoanalyst Fromm defines love as the act of giving of the self to another. Beyond this aspect of giving, he sees "certain basic elements, common to all forms of love. These are *care, responsibility, respect*, and *knowledge*."

Strategies: Definition, Classification/Division
Themes: Ethics/Values, Community

PAUL FUSSELL, ***The Boy Scout Handbook*** *(5 pp.)*

Fussell, a literary and social critic, analyzes and finds highly praiseworthy the 1979 edition of *The Official Boy Scout Handbook*. "Its good sense is not merely about swimming safely and putting campfires 'cold out.' The good sense is psychological and ethical as well. Indeed, this handbook is among the very few remaining popular repositories of something like classical ethics."

Strategies: Illustration, Argument and Persuasion
Themes: Ethics/Values, Coming of Age, Education

MARTIN GANSBERG, ***37 Who Saw Murder Didn't Call Police*** *(4 pp.)*

Reporter Gansberg describes the notorious 1963 murder of Kitty Genovese on the streets of Queens, New York, an incident that became a symbol of public apathy: "For more than half an hour 38 respectable, law-abiding citizens . . . watched a killer stalk and stab a woman in three separate attacks. . . . Not one person telephoned the police during the assault."

Strategy: Description
Themes: Ethics/Values, Community

HENRY LOUIS GATES JR., ***The Debate Has Been Miscast from the Start*** *(5 pp.)*

A scholar of African American literature, Gates argues for the value of multiculturalism: "Ours is a world that already is fissured by nationality, ethnicity, race, and gender. And the only way to transcend those divisions—to forge, for once, a civic culture that respects both differences and commonalities—is through education that seeks to comprehend the diversity of human culture."

Strategies: Definition, Illustration, Argument and Persuasion
Themes: Cultural Diversity, Education

HENRY LOUIS GATES JR., ***Joining the Church*** *(7 pp.)*

In this excerpt from his memoirs about growing up in a small West Virginia town in the 1950s, Gates remembers the role that churches and religion played in the lives of the closely-knit black residents: "What the church did provide was a sense of community, moments of intimacy, of belonging to a culture."

Strategies: Comparison/Contrast, Narration, Argument and Persuasion
Themes: Family, Places, Community

HENRY LOUIS GATES JR., ***Talking Black*** *(9 pp.)*

Gates, who has written many books about African American language, culture, and literary history, here urges African American scholars not to be confined by white traditions of literary criticism when examining African American works: "[W]e as critics can turn to our own peculiarly black structures of thought and feeling to develop our own language of criticism. We do so by drawing on the black vernacular, the language we use to speak to each other when no white people are around."

Strategies: Illustration, Metaphor, Argument and Persuasion
Themes: Cultural Diversity, Writing, Education

NATHAN GLAZER, ***Some Very Modest Proposals for the Improvement of American Education*** *(7 pp.)*

Sociologist Glazer suggests a number of low-cost changes to improve the performance of public schools. Above all, he emphasizes the primary importance of supporting professional teaching, seeing "the teacher, alone, up front, explaining, encouraging, guiding" as "the heart of the matter."

Strategies: Argument and Persuasion, Cause/Effect
Theme: Education

ELLEN GOODMAN, ***The Company Man*** *(3 pp.)*

Columnist Goodman tells a cautionary tale of a workaholic executive, obsessed with his job but a stranger to his wife and children, who meets an unhappy end: "He worked himself to death, finally and precisely, at 3:00 A.M. Sunday morning. The obituary didn't say that, of course. It said that he died of coronary thrombosis . . . but everyone among his friends and acquaintances knew it instantly."

Strategies: Definition, Narration, Analogy
Themes: Ethics/Values, Family, Work (and Play), Gender

STEPHEN JAY GOULD, ***Evolution as Fact and Theory*** *(8 pp.)*

Gould, a paleontologist and vocal critic of "scientific creationism," rejects creationist claims that biological evolution is just a "theory": "No biologist has been led to doubt the fact that evolution occurred; we are debating *how* it happened . . . Creationists pervert and caricature this debate by conveniently neglecting the common conviction that underlies it."

Strategies: Comparison/Contrast, Definition, Argument and Persuasion
Themes: Ethics/Values, Science

STEPHEN JAY GOULD, ***Our Allotted Lifetimes*** *(6 pp.)*

Gould makes several observations about the lifespans of different animals based on size and metabolism and concludes that, "Measured by the sensible internal clocks of their own hearts or the rhythm of their own breathing, all mammals live about the same time."

Strategies: Comparison/Contrast, Description
Themes: Ethics/Values, Science

STEPHEN JAY GOULD, ***Women's Brains*** *(5 pp.)*

Gould traces nineteenth-century scientists' efforts to measure differences in the weight of women's and men's brains and social planners' use of that data to justify social distinctions, especially in the kind and amount of education provided for women and men. He cautions, "I would rather label the whole enterprise of setting a biological value upon groups [such as women, blacks, and poor people] for what it is: irrelevant and highly injurious."

Strategies: Narration, Argument and Persuasion, Process Analysis
Themes: Politics/Government, Human/Civil Rights, Science

BOB GREENE, ***It Took This Night to Make Us Know*** *(3 pp.)*

Journalist Greene laments the persistence and vehemence of anti-Semitism evidenced in the murder of Israeli athletes at the Munich Olympics: "There is a hate for us that goes back centuries, and every time it seems to have weakened with the years there is another band of men ready to show us that the hate is still strong enough to make them kill in the night."

Strategy: Narration
Themes: Human/Civil Rights, Cultural Diversity

LANI GUINIER, ***The Tyranny of the Majority** (6 pp.)*

The first black woman to be a tenured professor at Harvard Law School, Constitutional scholar Guinier argues that "in a racially divided society, majority rule may be perceived as majority tyranny." For the current system of "winner-take-all majoritarianism," she offers an alternative: "Structuring decisionmaking to allow the minority a 'turn.'"

Strategies: Illustration, Analogy, Argument and Persuasion

Themes: Ethics/Values, Politics/Government, Cultural Diversity

DONALD HALL, ***Four Ways of Reading** (4 pp.)*

Poet Donald Hall classifies four types of reading, defining the highest type as literary reading, which engages our full sensibilities because "great literature, if we read it well, opens us up to the world, and makes us more sensitive to it, as if we acquired eyes that could see through things and ears that could hear smaller sounds."

Strategies: Illustration, Classfication/Division

Themes: Ethics/Values, Popular Culture, Writing, Education

EDWARD T. HALL, ***The Arab World** (9 pp.)*

An anthropologist noted for insightful cross-cultural studies, Hall is an expert in the field of proxemics, the analysis of cultural concepts of individual space. Here he describes how misunderstanding can arise between Westerners and Arabs because of the different rules that govern their interpersonal behavior; for example, "Arabs look each other in the eye when talking with an intensity that makes most Americans highly uncomfortable."

Strategies: Comparison/Contrast, Illustration, Classification/Division

Themes: Ethics/Values, Cultural Diversity

PETE HAMILL, ***Winning Isn't Everything** (5 pp.)*

Hamill, a journalist, argues against the popular conception of winning: "Just when we appear to have triumphed, we must stop like Sisyphus and again begin rolling the boulder up that mountain. The true athlete teaches us that winning isn't everything, but struggle is."

Strategies: Comparison/Contrast, Definition, Argument and Persuasion

Themes: Ethics/Values, Work (and Play)

SYDNEY J. HARRIS, ***A Jerk** (2 pp.)*

Newspaper columnist Harris defines a jerk as a person without self-awareness:

"All of us are egotists to some extent, but most of us—unlike the jerk—are perfectly and horribly aware of it when we make asses of ourselves. The jerk never knows."

Strategies: Comparison/Contrast, Definition
Themes: Ethics/Values

S. I. HAYAKAWA, ***How Dictionaries Are Made*** *(3 pp.)*

Hayakawa, a semanticist, explains the process through which dictionary definitions are created. Dictionary definitions, he insists, are not "authoritative statements about the 'true meanings' of words"; "we can be *guided* by the historical record afforded us by the dictionary, but we cannot be *bound* by it."

Strategy: Process Analysis
Themes: Writing, Education, Language

VICKI HEARNE, ***What's Wrong with Animal Rights?*** *(3 pp.)*

Hearne, a writer and animal trainer, criticizes many in the animal rights movement for not really understanding animals or their relationship to humans: "The question that needs to be asked . . . is not, do they have rights? or, what are those rights? but rather, what is a right?"

Strategies: Definition, Narration, Argument and Persuasion
Themes: Ethics/Values, Nature, Work (and Play)

WILLIAM LEAST HEAT-MOON, ***A List of Nothing in Particular*** *(4 pp.)*

By listing his detailed observations, writer William Least Heat-Moon demonstrates that a desert landscape, thought to contain "nothing," is actually quite full: "To say nothing is out here is incorrect; to say the desert is stingy with everything except space and light, stone and earth is closer to the truth."

Strategies: Description, Narration
Themes: Nature, Places

ERNEST HEMINGWAY, ***Camping Out*** *(4 pp.)*

Novelist Hemingway explains what one can do to make a camping trip both enjoyable and painless: "It is all right to talk about roughing it in the woods. But the real woodsman is the man who can be really comfortable in the bush."

Strategies: Narration, Process Analysis
Themes: Nature, Work (and Play)

NAT HENTOFF, ***Free Speech on Campus*** *(6 pp.)*

Journalist Hentoff argues against campus restrictions on racist, sexist, and other hateful forms of speech: "After all, if students are to be 'protected' from bad ideas, how are they going to learn to identify and cope with them? Sending such ideas underground simply makes them stronger and more dangerous."

Strategies: Illustration, Argument and Persuasion

Themes: Politics/Government, Cultural Diversity, Education

GILBERT HIGHET, ***The Gettysburg Address*** *(6 pp.)*

Scholar Highet analyzes Lincoln's "Gettysburg Address," providing a model of literary criticism: "It does not spoil such a work of art to analyze it as closely as we have done; it is altogether fitting and proper that we should do this: for it helps us to penetrate more deeply into the rich meaning of the Gettysburg Address, and it allows us the rare privilege of watching the workings of a great man's mind."

Strategies: Cause/Effect, Process Analysis

Themes: Politics/Government, Writing, Language

EDWARD HOAGLAND, ***The Courage of Turtles*** *(6 pp.)*

Nature writer Hoagland uses detailed, image-filled description to convey his deep admiration for turtles and his concern that human intervention in their natural environment has hurt their populations: "Creeping up the brooks to sad, constricted marshes, burdened as they are with that box on their backs, they're walking into a setup where all their enemies move thirty times faster than they. It's like the nightmare most of us have whimpered through."

Strategies: Description, Narration

Themes: Ethics/Values, Nature, Environment

LINDA HOGAN, ***Hearing Voices*** *(4 pp.)*

Hogan, a Chickasaw writer and conservationist, encourages readers to listen to the language of the earth, seeing in this almost mystical connection the seeds of poetry: "Sometimes, like the wind, poetry has its own laws speaking for the life of the planet. It is a language that wants to bring back together what the other words have torn apart. It is the language of life speaking through us about the sacredness of life."

Strategies: Illustration, Process Analysis

Themes: Ethics/Values, Cultural Diversity, Nature, Environment

JOHN HOLT, ***How Teachers Make Children Hate Reading*** *(8 pp.)*

Education advocate Holt challenges traditional methods of teaching reading that focus on vocabulary and right-or-wrong answers to comprehension questions. Rather, he argues teachers should make reading "an exciting, joyous adventure," encouraging students to "find something, dive into it, take the good parts, skip the bad parts, get what you can out of it, go on to something else."

Strategies: Narration, Argument and Persuasion
Themes: Writing, Education

BELL HOOKS, ***Teaching New Worlds/New Words*** *(7 pp.)*

Hooks, a feminist writer and social critic, presents a passionate meditation on standard English as "the oppressor's language" and argues that vernacular English helps create a "counter-hegemonic worldview": "It is absolutely essential that the revolutionary power of black vernacular speech not be lost in contemporary culture."

Strategies: Comparison/Contrast, Definition, Argument and Persuasion
Themes: Ethics/Values, Human/Civil Rights, Cultural Diversity, Language

SUE HUBBELL, ***The Beekeeper*** *(4 pp.)*

Naturalist Sue Hubbell describes the steps in the process of harvesting honey on her bee farm as well as the demands it requires: "Even a very strong young man works up a sweat wrapped in a bee suit in the heat, hustling sixty-pound supers while being harassed by angry bees. It is a hard job."

Strategies: Description, Narration, Process Analysis
Themes: Nature, Work (and Play)

LANGSTON HUGHES, ***Salvation*** *(3 pp.)*

Poet Hughes tells the autobiographical story of a coerced religious experience: "So I decided that maybe to save further trouble, I'd better lie, too, and say that Jesus had come, and get up and be saved."

Strategy: Narration
Themes: Ethics/Values, Family, Coming of Age

ZORA NEALE HURSTON, ***How It Feels to Be Colored Me*** *(4 pp.)*

Folklorist and writer Hurston embraces her racial identity: "But I am not tragically colored. There is no great sorrow dammed up in my soul . . . I do not belong to the sobbing school of Negrohood who hold that nature somehow has given them a lowdown dirty deal."

Strategies: Comparison/Contrast, Narration
Themes: Cultural Diversity, Coming of Age, Community

MOLLY IVINS, ***Living Wage Fight Goes On*** *(2 pp.)*

Texas journalist Ivins examines the controversy over raising the minimum wage, arguing that if Congress is unwilling to do so nationally, then municipalities should do so on a local level: "The premise is simple—you start by targeting city government with a requirement that any firm holding a service contract with the city pay enough . . . to get workers out of poverty. It's a concept, no?"

Strategies: Comparison/Contrast, Illustration, Argument and Persuasion
Themes: Ethics/Values, Politics/Government, Human/Civil Rights

PICO IYER, ***The Contagion of Innocence*** *(10 pp.)*

Iyer, a journalist and world traveler, considers the international appeal of American pop culture and the way images of America have come to symbolize the new internationalism: "Though Paris and Tokyo and Sydney and Toronto are all becoming natural meeting points for this multipolar culture, America is still the spiritual home of the very notion of integration: everyone feels at home in only two places, Milos Forman has said—at home, and in America."

Strategies: Illustration, Classification/Division
Themes: Cultural Diversity, Popular Culture, Work (and Play)

SUSAN JACOBY, ***Notes from a Free-Speech Junkie*** *(4 pp.)*

Journalist Jacoby ardently opposes feminist censorship of pornography. She dismisses the idea that "porn books, magazines, and movies pose a greater threat to women than similarly repulsive exercises of free speech pose to other offended groups" and concludes that "you can't OD on the First Amendment because free speech is its own best antidote."

Strategies: Illustration, Argument and Persuasion
Themes: Politics/Government, Popular Culture, Gender

THOMAS JEFFERSON, ***The Declaration of Independence*** *(4 pp.)*

The Declaration, a classic defense of democracy as the ideal form of government, is a deductive argument, based on the premise "that all men are created equal, that they are endowed by their Creator with certain unalienable Rights, that among these are Life, Liberty, and the pursuit of Happiness."

Strategies: Definition, Argument and Persuasion
Themes: Ethics/Values, Politics/Government, Human/Civil Rights

SAMUEL JOHNSON, ***On Self-Love and Indolence*** *(5 pp.)*

Eighteenth-century writer and raconteur Samuel Johnson points out the common human failure to deal with one's faults: "There is, perhaps, no man, however hardened by impudence or dissipated by levity, sheltered by hypocrisy, or blasted by disgrace, who does not intend some time to review his conduct, and to regulate the remainder of his life by the laws of virtue."

Strategies: Definition, Cause/Effect
Themes: Ethics/Values

MICHIKO KAKUTANI, ***The Word Police*** *(6 pp.)*

Kakutani, critic and cultural commentator, attacks "the excesses of the word police": "In the case of the politically correct, the prohibition of certain words, phrases, and ideas is advanced in the cause of building a brave new world free of racism and hate, but this vision of harmony clashes with the very ideals of diversity and inclusion . . . and it's purchased at the cost of freedom of speech."

Strategies: Illustration, Classification/Division, Argument and Persuasion
Themes: Ethics/Values, Politics, Language

GARRISON KEILLOR, ***How to Write a Personal Letter*** *(3 pp.)*

Keillor, a writer and radio humorist, offers advice for overcoming the barriers we face in letting other people know us through our writing: "Make mistakes and plunge on . . . Outrage, confusion, love—whatever is in your mind, let it find a way to the page."

Strategies: Process Analysis, Argument and Persuasion
Themes: Writing, Community

MARTIN LUTHER KING JR., ***I Have a Dream*** *(4 pp.)*

Dr. King, America's most influential twentieth century civil rights leader, delivered this stirring speech at the Lincoln Memorial to promote passage of the 1964 Civil Rights Act and the Voting Rights Act of 1965. "I have a dream," he says, in an eloquent listing of his visions for the future, "that my four little children will one day live in a nation where they will not be judged by the color of their skin but by the content of their character."

Strategies: Comparison/Contrast, Description, Argument and Persuasion
Themes: Ethics/Values, Politics/Government, Human/Civil Rights, Community

MARTIN LUTHER KING JR., ***Letter from Birmingham Jail*** *(13 pp.)*

Jailed for leading a demonstration against segregation and discrimination, clergyman and civil rights leader King wrote this 1963 letter in response to criticism from white moderates: "I submit that an individual who breaks a law that conscience tells him is unjust, and who willingly accepts the penalty of imprisonment in order to arouse the conscience of the community over its injustice, is in reality expressing the highest respect for law."

Strategies: Comparison/Contrast, Definition, Argument and Persuasion

Themes: Ethics/Values, Politics/Government, Human/Civil Rights, Community

STEPHEN KING, ***Why We Crave Horror Movies*** *(3 pp.)*

King, best-selling horror novelist and screenwriter, believes we all feel "anticivilization emotions" that demand "periodic exercise"—and get it in horror movies. Watching them, "we are daring the nightmare."

Strategies: Definition, Analogy

Themes: Ethics/Values, Popular Culture, Work (and Play)

BARBARA KINGSOLVER, ***Stone Soup*** *(8 pp.)*

Kingsolver, a novelist and journalist, argues against the idea that "family" should be defined only in the most narrowly traditional sense: "Divorce, remarriage, single parenthood, gay parents, and blended families simply are. They're facts of our time."

Strategies: Comparison/Contrast, Definition, Illustration, Argument and Persuasion

Themes: Ethics/Values, Family

MAXINE HONG KINGSTON, ***No Name Woman*** *(11 pp.)*

Kingston mixes autobiography and fiction in her explorations of the multiple identities Chinese Americans achieve. Here she draws upon her mother, who "talks story," to explore what her No Name Aunt might contribute to her own self-understanding: "My aunt haunts me—her ghost drawn to me because now, after fifty years of neglect, I alone devote pages of paper to her."

Strategies: Narration, Cause/Effect

Themes: Cultural Diversity, Family, Places, Coming of Age

MAXINE HONG KINGSTON, ***On Discovery*** *(2 pp.)*

Kingston, a Chinese American novelist and nonfiction writer, protests traditional female roles in this gender-bending parable from *China Men*: "One day his attendants changed his gold hoops to jade studs and strapped his feet to shoes that curved like bridges. They plucked out each hair on his face, powdered him white, painted his eyebrows like a moth's wings, painted his cheeks and lips red."

Strategies: Comparison/Contrast, Analogy, Definition
Themes: Cultural Diversity, Gender

PERRI KLASS, ***Learning the Language*** *(4 **pp.**)*

Dr. Klass analyzes the jargon and abbreviated forms of language she learned as a medical student, some of which are ironically, even painfully, irreverent: "By reformulating a patient's pain and problems into a language that the patient doesn't even speak, I suppose we are in some sense taking those pains and problems under our jurisdiction and also reducing their emotional impact."

Strategies: Comparison/Contrast, Definition, Satire
Themes: Ethics/Values, Coming of Age, Education, Language

EDWARD I. KOCH, ***Death and Justice: How Capital Punishment Affirms Life*** *(6 **pp.**)*

Ed Koch, the outspoken three-term mayor of New York City, rejects arguments against the death penalty: "When opponents of capital punishment say to the state, 'I will not let you kill in my name,' they are also saying to murderers: 'You can kill in your *own* name as long as I have an excuse for not getting involved.'"

Strategies: Definition, Argument and Persuasion, Cause/Effect
Themes: Ethics/Values, Human/Civil Rights, Community

WILLIAM KOWINSKI, ***Kids in the Mall: Growing Up Controlled*** *(5 **pp.**)*

Kowinski, a journalist, analyzes the shopping mall as a hangout for American youth, as well as its effects, for better and for worse: "It's here that these kids get their street sense, only it's mall sense. They are learning the ways of a large-scale artificial environment: its subtleties and flexibilities, its particular pleasures and resonances, and the attitudes it fosters."

Strategies: Definition, Illustration, Argument and Persuasion
Themes: Ethics/Values, Family

JONATHAN KOZOL, ***The Human Cost of an Illiterate Society*** *(8 **pp.**)*

Sociologist Kozol decries the appallingly high rate of illiteracy in the United States and details the many ways people who can't read are disenfranchised and endangered: "Choice, in almost all of its facets, is diminished in the life of an illiterate adult. Even the printed TV schedule, which provides most people with the luxury of preselection, does not belong within the arsenal of options in illiterate existence."

Strategies: Definition, Narration, Argument and Persuasion
Themes: Ethics/Values, Coming of Age, Work (and Play), Education

CHARLES KRAUTHAMMER, ***The Just Wage: From Bad to Worth*** *(6 pp.)*

Political columnist Krauthammer argues against measurements of "comparable worth," the doctrine according to which "low-paying female-dominated jobs, like nursing, are worth as much (to employers or society) as 'comparable' male-dominated jobs, like plumbing, and that therefore by right and by law they should be paid the same."

Strategies: Comparison/Contrast, Classification/Division, Argument and Persuasion
Themes: Ethics/Values, Politics/Government, Work (and Play)

JOSEPH WOOD KRUTCH, ***The Most Dangerous Predator*** *(10 pp.)*

Critic and nature writer Krutch, one of twentieth-century America's leading intellectuals, in this essay counters pro-hunting arguments that all animals are predatory: "Nature's far from simple plan does depend upon a coexistence. Man is, on the other hand, the only animal who habitually exhausts or exterminates what he has learned to exploit."

Strategies: Definition, Description, Argument and Persuasion
Themes: Ethics/Values, Nature, Popular Culture, Work (and Play)

ELISABETH KÜBLER-ROSS, ***On the Fear of Death*** *(8 pp.)*

Psychiatrist Kübler-Ross writes about the psychological responses to dying: "Death is still a fearful, frightening happening, and the fear of death is a universal fear even if we think we have mastered it on many levels."

Strategies: Definition, Illustration, Argument and Persuasion
Themes: Ethics/Values, Science

THOMAS KUHN, ***The Route to Normal Science*** *(10 pp.)*

Physicist Kuhn explains the process by which any scientific field of study moves from competing theories to the emergence of a workable paradigm and the result of such paradigms: "Men whose research is based on shared paradigms are committed to the same rules and standards for scientific practice. That commitment and the apparent consensus it produces are prerequisites for normal science, i.e., for the genesis and continuation of a particular research tradition."

Strategies: Definition, Illustration
Theme: Science

BARBARA LAWRENCE, ***Four-Letter Words Can Hurt You*** *(3 pp.)*

With tact and thoughtfulness, Lawrence, a linguist, examines obscene language to illustrate how such words affect our concept of human activity: "Not all obscene words, of course, are . . . implicitly sadistic or denigrating to women . . . but all that I know do seem to serve a similar purpose: to reduce the human organism (especially the female organism) and human functions (especially sexual and procreative) to their least organic, most mechanical dimension."

Strategies: Illustration, Analogy, Argument and Persuasion
Themes: Ethics/Values, Gender, Language

JOHN LEO, ***Journalese as a Second Language*** *(4 pp.)*

Conservative journalist and columnist John Leo exposes his profession's linguistic foibles—including euphemisms, clichés, and sexist language. "Much of the difficulty in mastering journalese," writes Leo, "comes from its slight overlap with English."

Strategies: Definition, Illustration, Satire
Themes: Popular Culture, Language

DORIS LESSING, ***My Father*** *(8 pp.)*

Novelist Lessing explores the life of her father, whom she knew when "his best years were over": "The people I've met, particularly the women, who knew him young, speak of his high spirits, his energy, his enjoyment of life. . . . I do not think these people would have easily recognized the ill, irritable, abstracted, hypochondriac man I knew."

Strategies: Description, Narration, Cause/Effect
Themes: Family, Community

MICHAEL LEVIN, ***The Case for Torture*** *(3 pp.)*

Levin, a philosophy professor whose ideas have generated great controversy, argues that "there are situations in which torture is not merely permissible but morally mandatory."

Strategies: Illustration, Argument and Persuasion
Themes: Ethics/Values

C. S. LEWIS, ***We Have No "Right to Happiness"*** *(5 pp.)*

Lewis, considered the most influential Christian writer of the late twentieth century, argues against the view that people have an unlimited right to happiness, particularly in terms of sexual fulfillment: "Every unkindness and breach of faith seems to be condoned provided that the object aimed at is 'four bare legs in a bed.'"

Strategies: Definition, Analogy, Satire
Themes: Ethics/Values

ABRAHAM LINCOLN, ***The Gettysburg Address*** *(2 pp.)*

President Lincoln's classic speech dedicating the Gettysburg battlefield as a memorial to the thousands killed in the Civil War, attempts to subdue the wrath of both sides and preserve the Union, so that the "government of the people, by the people, for the people, shall not perish from the earth."

Strategies: Definition, Illustration
Themes: Ethics/Values, Politics/Government, Human/Civil Rights

BARRY LOPEZ, ***My Horse*** *(6 pp.)*

Known for his nature essays, Lopez is intrigued as much by human nature as by the natural world: "I do not own a horse. I am attached to a truck, however, and I have come to think of it in a similar way. It has no name; it never occurred to me to give it a name. It has little decoration; neither of us is partial to decoration."

Strategy: Metaphor
Themes: Nature, Popular Culture

BARRY LOPEZ, ***A Passage of the Hands*** *(9 pp.)*

In this autobiographical essay, Lopez evokes memory through an intense examination of his hands: "They remember all they have done, all that has happened to them, the ways in which they have been surprised or worked themselves free of desperate trouble, or lost their grip and so caused harm."

Strategies: Narration, Analogy
Themes: Ethics/Values, Family, Work (and Play)

WILLIAM LUTZ, ***The World of Doublespeak*** *(7 pp.)*

Lutz, an English professor and linguist, defines doublespeak as a "language that makes the bad seem good, the negative appear positive, the unpleasant appear attractive or at least tolerable."

Strategies: Definition, Illustration, Classification/Division
Themes: Ethics/Values, Politics/Government, Language

NICCOLÒ MACHIAVELLI, ***The Morals of the Prince*** *(8 pp.)*

Machiavelli, political analyst and writer of the Italian Renaissance, offers advice to princes, whose chief duty, he says, is to preserve the state: "Any man who tries to be good all the time is bound to come to ruin among the great number who are not good. Hence a prince who wants to keep his post must learn how not to be good, and use that knowledge, or refrain from using it, as necessity requires."

Strategies: Classification, Argument and Persuasion, Cause/Effect
Themes: Ethics/Values, Politics/Government, Community

NANCY MAIRS, ***On Being a Cripple*** *(11 pp.)*

Mairs, whose autobiographical books reflect the physical and emotional challenges of coping with multiple sclerosis and other illnesses, rejects society's polite terms for disability: "I am a cripple. I choose this word to name me. . . . As a cripple, I swagger."

Strategies: Definition, Narration, Argument and Persuasion
Themes: Ethics/Values, Human/Civil Rights

MALCOLM X, ***Coming to an Awareness of Language*** *(3 pp.)*

Black Muslim activist and founder of the Organization of Afro-American Unity, Malcolm X describes his efforts while in prison to learn to read by copying the dictionary: "I suppose it was inevitable that as my word-base broadened, I could for the first time pick up a book and read and now begin to understand what the book was saying. Anyone who has read a great deal can imagine the new world that opened."

Strategies: Definition, Narration
Themes: Education, Language

JOYCE MAYNARD, ***An 18-Year-Old Looks Back on Life*** *(9 pp.)*

A Yale University freshman writing for the *New York Times Magazine* in 1972, Maynard characterizes her generation as self-indulgent and directionless, with nothing to aspire to or struggle against: "The fact that we set such a premium on being cool reveals a lot about my generation; the idea is not to care."

Strategies: Comparison/Contrast, Narration
Themes: Popular Culture, Coming of Age

BILL MCKIBBEN, ***Nature and Televised Nature*** *(11 pp.)*

Ecologist McKibben analyzes the artificiality of nature programs on television:

"Like urban living, TV cuts us off from context—stops us from understanding plants and animals as parts of systems, from grounding them in ideas larger than 'fresh' or fierce or cute."

Strategies: Comparison/Contrast, Illustration, Argument and Persuasion
Themes: Ethics/Values, Science, Nature, Popular Culture

JOHN MCMURTRY, ***Kill 'Em! Crush 'Em! Eat 'Em Raw!*** *(7 pp.)*

McMurtry—professional football player turned philosophy professor—turns a critical eye toward the culture of violence that surrounds football: "One difference between war and football, though, is that there is little or no protest against football."

Strategies: Comparison/Contrast, Analogy
Themes: Ethics/Values, Popular Culture

JOHN MCPHEE, ***The Pine Barrens*** *(7 pp.)*

A literary journalist, McPhee describes the vast Pine Barrens of central New Jersey, a "forest land that is still so undeveloped that it can be called wilderness," and his encounter with some people who live in the isolation of this wilderness.

Strategies: Description, Narration, Cause/Effect
Themes: Nature, Environment, Places

MARGARET MEAD, ***Can the American Family Survive?*** *(10 pp.)*

As a cultural anthropologist, Mead studied families from Nebraska to Samoa. In this essay she calls for federal programs to reduce the stresses on families and urges readers to think about "how people who have too little to do can help those who are burdened by too much."

Strategies: Comparison/Contrast, Argument and Persuasion, Cause/Effect
Themes: Politics/Government, Family, Community

MARY E. MEBANE, ***Shades of Black*** *(5 pp.)*

Teacher, playwright, and autobiographer Mebane recalls discrimination among African Americans at her college, where "social class and color were the primary criteria used in determining status on the campus," and her determination "to do not only well but better than my light-skinned peers."

Strategies: Narration, Classification/Division, Cause/Effect
Themes: Human/Civil Rights, Education

H. L. Mencken, ***The Libido for the Ugly*** *(4 pp.)*

Early twentieth-century satirist and cultural critic Mencken writes scathingly about towns along the railroad lines of western Pennsylvania and draws a larger point about American taste: "Here is something that the psychologists have so far neglected: the love of ugliness for its own sake, the lust to make the world intolerable."

Strategies: Description, Satire, Argument and Persuasion
Theme: Places

Casey Miller and Kate Swift, ***Who's in Charge of the English Language?*** *(7 pp.)*

Miller and Swift, pioneers in the study of gender-biased language, argue in this 1990 paper that recognizing the extent to which traditional language usage has marginalized women is the first step in achieving gender-neutral language: "Linguistic changes spring from nothing less than new perceptions of the world and of ourselves."

Strategies: Definition, Classification/Division, Cause/Effect
Themes: Ethics/Values, Gender, Education, Language

Jessica Mitford, ***Behind the Formaldehyde Curtain*** *(8 pp.)*

Muckraking social analyst Mitford attacks the practices of the American funeral industry: "The drama begins . . . at the mortuary," where the body "is in short order sprayed, sliced, pierced, pickled, trussed, trimmed, creamed, waxed, painted, rouged, and neatly dressed—transformed from a common corpse into a Beautiful Memory Picture."

Strategies: Satire, Argument and Persuasion, Process Analysis
Themes: Ethics/Values, Popular Culture

N. Scott Momaday, ***The Way to Rainy Mountain*** *(6 pp.)*

Combining history, legend, and autobiography, poet and essayist N. Scott Momaday traces the migration of the Kiowa people through the life story of his paternal grandmother: "Although my grandmother lived out her long life in the shadow of Rainy Mountain, the immense landscape of the continental interior lay like memory in her blood."

Strategies: Narration, Metaphor
Themes: Ethics/Values, Cultural Diversity, Family, Places

Lance Morrow, ***What Is the Point of Working?*** *(6 pp.)*

A *Time* reporter and essayist, Morrow traces the decline of America's work ethic but reaffirms the value of even the most menial work: "Work is the way that we tend the world, the way that people connect. It is the most vigorous, vivid sign of life—in individuals and in civilizations."

Strategies: Definition, Narration, Argument and Persuasion
Themes: Ethics/Values, Community, Work (and Play)

DONALD M. MURRAY, ***The Maker's Eye: Revising Your Own Manuscripts*** ***(9 pp.)***

Murray, a writer and writing teacher, provides excerpts from earlier drafts of this essay to demonstrate the importance of revision: "Rewriting isn't virtuous. It isn't something that ought to be done. It is simply something that most writers find they have to do to discover what they have to say and how to say it. It is a condition of the writer's life."

Strategies: Definition, Process Analysis
Themes: Writing, Education

GLORIA NAYLOR, ***Mommy, What Does "Nigger" Mean?*** ***(4 pp.)***

Novelist Naylor recalls the first time she was called "nigger" by a white grade school classmate and contrasts its meaning in that context with the ways the word was used within her own family: "[T]he people in my grandmother's living room took a word that whites used to signify worthlessness or degradation and rendered it impotent."

Strategies: Comparison/Contrast, Illustration, Argument and Persuasion
Themes: Ethics/Values, Family, Language

ALLEEN PACE NILSEN, ***Sexism in English: Embodiment and Language*** ***(12 pp.)***

Nilsen, a professor of linguistics and children's literature, provides numerous examples of sexist language gleaned from dictionaries, etiquette books, myths, and elsewhere. She concludes that "sexism is not something existing independently in American English or in the particular dictionary that I happened to read. Rather, it exists in people's minds."

Strategies: Definition, Classification/Division
Themes: Ethics/Values, Gender, Language

JOYCE CAROL OATES, ***Against Nature*** ***(8 pp.)***

One of America's most prolific novelists and critics, Oates recalls an encounter with the inevitability of mortality after suffering a heart attack while jogging:

"When you discover yourself lying on the ground, limp and unresisting, head in the dirt, and helpless, the earth seems to shift forward as a presence; hard, emphatic, not mere surface but a genuine force—there is no other word for it but *presence*."

Strategies: Narration, Analogy

Themes: Ethics/Values, Nature, Coming of Age

GEORGE ORWELL, ***A Hanging*** *(5 pp.)*

British writer Orwell recalls witnessing the hanging of a prisoner when he served as a member of the police force in colonial Burma. "He and we were a party of men walking together, seeing, hearing, feeling, understanding the same world; and in two minutes, with a sudden snap, one of us would be gone—one mind less, one world less."

Strategies: Definition, Illustration

Themes: Ethics/Values, Politics/Government, Human/Civil Rights, Community

GEORGE ORWELL, ***Marrakech*** *(6 pp.)*

In several stark, precision snapshots of characteristic Moroccan scenes, focusing on colonized people starving and barely alive, Orwell presents the dehumanizing effects of British colonial imperialism before World War II: "It is always difficult to believe that you are walking among human beings. All colonial empires are . . . founded upon that fact."

Strategies: Definition, Narration, Argument and Persuasion

Themes: Ethics/Values, Politics/Government, Writing

GEORGE ORWELL, ***Politics and the English Language*** *(12 pp.)*

Writing at the end of World War II, Orwell analyzes the "bad habits" that make writing "ugly and inaccurate." He goes on to advise writers to strive for clarity, directness, and honesty based on six simple rules, such as "Never use a long word where a short one will do."

Strategies: Definition, Illustration, Process Analysis

Themes: Ethics/Values, Politics/Government, Writing, Language

GEORGE ORWELL, ***Shooting an Elephant*** *(7 pp.)*

Here Orwell recalls a moment of revelation when, as a colonial policeman, he—egged on by a hostile crowd of natives—reluctantly killed an elephant: "I perceived in this moment that when the white man turns tyrant it is his own freedom that he destroys."

Strategies: Definition, Narration, Process Analysis

Themes: Ethics/Values, Politics/Government, Human/Civil Rights, Coming of Age, Community

GEORGE ORWELL, ***Why I Write*** *(6 pp.)*

Novelist and essayist Orwell traces his development as a writer and identifies his particular role as a political writer: "I write . . . because there is some lie that I want to expose, some fact to which I want to draw attention."

Strategies: Illustration, Narration, Process Analysis

Themes: Ethics/Values, Politics/Government, Writing, Work (and Play), Language

CYNTHIA OZICK, ***A Drugstore Eden*** *(11 pp.)*

Recalling her Depression childhood in the Bronx, Ozick describes reading in the sheltered "Eden" of her mother's garden while her parents pursued the American Dream in the Park View Pharmacy: "Mostly, the books came from the Travelling Library; inside my hammock cave the melting glue of new bindings sent out a blissful redolence."

Strategies: Description, Narration, Analogy

Themes: Family, Coming of Age, Work (and Play)

CYNTHIA OZICK, ***A Drugstore in Winter*** *(7 pp.)*

Ozick's lyrical reflections on growing up—and discovering the world of books—in her parents' Bronx drugstore in the 1930s ends on a melancholy note: "And then one day you find yourself leaning here, writing at that selfsame round glass table salvaged from the Park View Pharmacy—writing this, an impossibility, a summary of how you came to be where you are now, and where, God knows, is that?"

Strategies: Narration, Analogy, Metaphor

Themes: Family, Writing, Coming of Age, Work

CAMILLE PAGLIA, ***Rape: A Bigger Danger than Feminists Know*** *(5 pp.)*

Paglia, a social critic who has generated much controversy, argues that because males are natural sexual predators, the whole idea of "date rape" is the result of feminists not accepting reality: "A girl who lets herself get dead drunk at a fraternity party is a fool. A girl who goes upstairs alone with a brother at a fraternity party is an idiot. Feminists call this 'blaming the victim.' I call it common sense."

Strategies: Comparison/Contrast, Argument and Persuasion
Themes: Ethics/Values, Community, Gender

JO GOODWIN PARKER, ***What Is Poverty? (5 pp.)***

Parker paints a graphic, arresting portrait of the desperate character of poverty: "Poverty is living in a smell that never leaves . . . a smell of urine, sour milk, and spoiling food. . . . Poverty is being tired. I have always been tired."

Strategies: Definition, Illustration, Argument and Persuasion
Themes: Ethics/Values, Community

NOEL PERRIN, ***Forever Virgin: The American View of America (10 pp.)***

Environmentalist and essayist Perrin here traces Americans' four-hundred year history of exploring and conquering the wilderness: "For the first two centuries that Europeans lived in North America, they saw the continent as a . . . vast, powerful, and immensely rich wilderness, which it would be the bounden duty of their descendants to turn into farms and gardens and alabaster cities."

Strategies: Comparison/Contrast, Description
Themes: Ethics/Values, Nature, Environment

ALEXANDER PETRUNKEVITCH, ***The Spider and the Wasp (5 pp.)***

Petrunkevitch, an eminent zoologist, explains the process by which the female digger wasp turns a living tarantula into a nursery as well as nourishment for one of her eggs: "It is a classic example of what looks like intelligence pitted against instinct—a strange situation in which the victim, though fully able to defend itself, submits unwittingly to its destruction."

Strategies: Comparison/Contrast, Definition, Process Analysis
Themes: Science, Nature

PLATO, ***The Allegory of the Cave (5 pp.)***

In this classic dialogue between Socrates and a companion, Plato explores the nature of human knowledge and understanding: the difference between flawed sensory perception and a larger perception of "ideal" truth. "My opinion is that in the world of knowledge the idea of good appears last of all, and is seen only with an effort; and, when seen, is also inferred to be the universal author of all things beautiful and right."

Strategies: Definition, Analogy, Cause/Effect
Themes: Ethics/Values, Politics/Government

KATHA POLLITT, ***Does a Literary Canon Matter?* (7 *pp.*)**

Poet and essayist Pollitt weighs conservative and liberal views of what should constitute the literary canon taught in schools. For all sides, she notes, the "chief end of reading is to produce a desirable kind of person and a desirable kind of society."

Strategies: Definition, Classification/Division, Cause/Effect
Themes: Popular Culture, Writing

NEIL POSTMAN, ***Future Shlock* (10 *pp.*)**

A radical reformer of education since the 1970s, Postman cautions that electronic media trivialize our political discourse by substituting sound bites and talk-show tactics for sustained conversation and deliberation: "As a medium for conducting public business, language has receded in importance; it has been moved to periphery of culture and has been replaced at the center by the entertaining visual image."

Strategies: Comparison/Contrast, Description, Argument and Persuasion
Themes: Politics/Government, Popular Culture, Language

ANNA QUINDLEN, ***Homeless* (3 *pp.*)**

A Pulitzer Prize-winning columnist and best-selling novelist, Quindlen asks readers to consider the world of the homeless in concrete terms: "They are not the homeless. They are people with no homes. No drawer that holds the spoons. No windows to look out upon the world. My God. That is everything."

Strategies: Comparison/Contrast, Definition, Description
Themes: Ethics/Values, Popular Culture, Places

ROBERT RAMÌREZ, ***The Barrio* (4 *pp.*)**

Ramìrez, a television newsman, characterizes the essence of the Chicano enclave, the barrio: "The feeling of family, a rare and treasurable sentiment, pervades and accounts for the inability of the people to leave. The barrio is this attitude manifested on the countenances of the people, on the faces of their homes, and in the gaiety of their gardens."

Strategies: Definition, Description
Themes: Ethics/Values, Cultural Diversity, Work (and Play)

WILLIAM RASPBERRY, ***The Handicap of Definition* (3 *pp.*)**

A Pulitzer Prize-winning columnist, African American Raspberry asks, "Wouldn't it be wonderful if we could infect black children with the notion that excellence in math is 'black' rather than white, or possibly Chinese?" He advocates "the importance of developing positive ethnic traditions."

Strategies: Comparison/Contrast, Definition, Argument and Persuasion
Themes: Human/Civil Rights, Education

ISHMAEL REED, ***America: The Multinational Society*** *(5 pp.)*

Reed, whose provocative poems, novels, and essays explore the African American aesthetic, reminds readers that Adolf Hitler was "the archetypal monoculturalist." For Reed, multiculturalism strengthens American society, making it "a place where the cultures of the world crisscross. This is possible because the United States is unique in the world: The world is here."

Strategies: Definition, Satire, Cause/Effect
Themes: Cultural Diversity, Community

ROBERT B. REICH, ***Why the Rich Are Getting Richer and the Poor Poorer*** *(8 pp.)*

Economist Reich explains current income differentials in the United States based on how one's job functions within the new global economy: Those who work with information, "data, words, and oral and visual symbols . . . are in high demand around the whole world [which] ensures that their salaries are quite high."

Strategies: Definition, Metaphor, Cause/Effect
Themes: Work (and Play)

JEREMY RIFKIN, ***The Age of Simulation*** *(10 pp.)*

Rifkin, a social policy critic, analyzes with alarm a pervasive contemporary phenomenon—the substitution of simulated experience for reality, first through television and now through virtual reality and other electronic means: "The substitution of artificial experiences for natural ones masks an almost pathological fear of the living world."

Strategies: Definition, Illustration, Argument and Persuasion
Themes: Ethics/Values, Science

PAUL ROBERTS, ***How to Say Nothing in Five Hundred Words*** *(12 pp.)*

In this 1958 essay Roberts, a professor of English and linguistics, offers lighthearted but practical advice for student writers: "Don't worry too much about figuring out what the instructor thinks about the subject so that you can cuddle up with him. Chances are his views are no stronger than yours."

Strategies: Description, Satire, Process Analysis
Themes: Writing, Education

RICHARD RODRIGUEZ, ***Aria: A Memoir of a Bilingual Childhood*** ***(12 pp.)***

In this highly personal account of growing up the son of Mexican immigrants, Rodriguez makes a case against bilingual education: "[Spanish] was a ghetto language that deepened and strengthened my feeling of public separateness. What I needed to learn in school was that I had the right, and the obligation, to speak the public language."

Strategies: Definition, Narration
Themes: Cultural Diversity, Coming of Age, Education, Language

RICHARD RODRIGUEZ, ***None of This Is Fair*** ***(5 pp.)***

Mexican American Rodriguez recalls his own strong ambivalence over being the beneficiary of affirmation action after a fellow grad student who had received one job offer to the many presented to Rodriguez challenged him. "His words stung me: there was nothing he was telling me that I didn't know. I had admitted everything already."

Strategies: Definition, Narration, Argument and Persuasion
Themes: Politics/Government, Cultural Diversity, Coming of Age, Education

BETTY ROLLIN, ***Motherhood: Who Needs It?*** ***(11 pp.)***

Columnist and news correspondent Rollin, writing in 1970, takes the then-controversial stance that motherhood ought not to be "culturally compulsory": "It doesn't make sense anymore to pretend that women need babies . . . If God were still speaking to us in a voice we could hear, even He would probably say, 'Be fruitful. Don't multiply.'"

Strategies: Description, Narration, Satire, Cause/Effect
Themes: Nature, Family, Work (and Play), Gender

ANDY ROONEY, ***In and of Ourselves We Trust*** ***(2 pp.)***

Rooney, a columnist and television commentator, recounts his refusal to run a red light on a deserted highway in the middle of the night. Pondering his action, he decides "I think I stopped because it's part of a contract we all have with each other. It's not only the law, but it's an agreement we have, and we trust each other to honor it."

Strategies: Definition, Narration, Argument and Persuasion
Themes: Ethics/Values, Community

MIKE ROSE, *"I Just Wanna Be Average"* (8 pp.)

Rose, a professor of education at UCLA, explains the deadening effect of high school vocational education on himself and his fellow classmates. These students "protect themselves from such suffocating madness by taking on with a vengeance the identity implied in the vocational track. Reject the confusion and frustration by openly defining yourself as the Common Joe."

Strategies: Narration, Cause/Effect, Process Analysis
Themes: Ethics/Values, Cultural Diversity, Coming of Age, Education

BERTRAND RUSSELL, *A Free Man's Worship* (8 pp.)

One of the twentieth century's most influential mathematicians and philosophers, Lord Russell explains in this excerpt from *Mysticism and Logic* that in the face of God's and Nature's indifference, humane sympathy is justified: "In this lies Man's true freedom: in determination to worship only the God created by our own love of the good, to respect only the heaven which inspires the insight of our best moments."

Strategies: Definition, Analogy, Cause/Effect
Themes: Ethics/Values

BERTRAND RUSSELL, *The Study of Mathematics* (3 pp.)

An influential mathematician and philosopher of the twentieth century, Lord Russell in this excerpt from *Mysticism and Logic* justifies the study of mathematics, not for its practical usefulness but for its "beauty cold and austere, like that of sculpture, without appeal to any part of our weaker nature, without the gorgeous trappings of painting or music, yet sublimely pure, and capable of a stern perfection such as only the greatest art can show."

Strategies: Comparison/Contrast, Definition, Argument and Persuasion
Themes: Ethics/Values, Science

SCOTT RUSSELL SANDERS, *The Inheritance of Tools* (7 pp.)

Writer Sanders sees inherited tools, and the craftsmanship they imply, as a metaphor for the transmission of his family's values: "A house will stand, a table will bear weight, the sides of a box will hold together, only if the joints are square and the members upright."

Strategies: Narration, Metaphor
Themes: Ethics/Values, Family, Community

SCOTT RUSSELL SANDERS, ***Under the Influence: Paying the Price of My Father's Booze*** ***(12 pp.)***

Writer Sanders here explores unsentimentally what it was like to grow up with—and to be the adult son of—an alcoholic father: "I am only trying to understand the corrosive mixture of helplessness, responsibility, and shame that I learned to feel as the son of an alcoholic."

Strategies: Definition, Narration

Themes: Ethics/Values, Family, Coming of Age

MAY SARTON, ***The Rewards of Living a Solitary Life*** ***(2 pp.)***

Sarton, a poet and novelist, believed that "alone one is never lonely." Instead, solitude allows one to sort out experiences and absorb what renews and rewards: "Solitude is the salt of personhood. It brings out the authentic flavor of every experience."

Strategies: Definition, Narration, Metaphor

Themes: Ethics/Values

JEAN-PAUL SARTRE, ***Existentialism*** ***(10 pp.)***

Sartre, philosopher and leading French twentieth century intellectual, defines existential philosophy, based on the premise that "when we say that a man is responsible for himself, we do not only mean that he is responsible for his own individuality, but that he is responsible for all men."

Strategies: Definition, Illustration

Themes: Ethics/Values, Community

ARTHUR M. SCHLESINGER JR., ***The Cult of Ethnicity, Good and Bad*** ***(3 pp.)***

Schlesinger, a noted historian, warns against pressing the "cult of ethnicity" too far: "The United States escaped the divisiveness of a multiethnic society by a brilliant solution: the creation of a brand-new national identity. The point of America was not to preserve old cultures but to forge a new *American* culture."

Strategies: Illustration, Classification/Division, Cause/Effect

Themes: Politics/Government, Cultural Diversity

CHIEF SEATTLE, ***Address*** ***(3 pp.)***

Chief Seattle's 1855 speech is a statement of peace and resignation, an elegy for the Northwest Indians' disappearance as they face removal to a reservation:

"Your time of decay may be distant, but it will surely come, for even the White Man whose God walked and talked with him as friend to friend, cannot be exempt from the common destiny. We may be brothers after all."

Strategies: Comparison/Contrast, Metaphor
Themes: Ethics/Values, Cultural Diversity, Community

RICHARD SELZER, ***The Knife*** *(8 pp.)*

A surgeon and acclaimed essayist, Selzer lyrically describes the most delicate operating room procedures: "So close is the joining of knife and surgeon that they are like the Centaur—the knife, below, all equine energy, the surgeon, above, with his delicate art."

Strategies: Metaphor, Process Analysis
Themes: Ethics/Values, Science

GAIL SHEEHY, ***Predictable Crises of Adulthood*** *(8 pp.)*

Acclaimed journalist and essayist Sheehy identifies four main "passages," or age-related crises in our lives that signal the necessity for personal change: "With each passage from one stage of human growth to the next, we . . . must shed a protective structure."

Strategies: Description, Illustration, Classification/Division
Theme: Popular Culture

LESLIE MARMON SILKO, ***Fences Against Freedom*** *(10 pp.)*

Recalling her experiences as a person of mixed Native American and white heritage, Silko reflects on issues of race and racism in the United States. "For miles before I approach the INS check stations, I can feel the anxiety pressing hard against my chest. But I feel anger too, a deep, abiding anger at the U. S. government."

Strategies: Definition, Illustration, Argument and Persuasion
Themes: Human/Civil Rights, Cultural Diversity, Community

PETER SINGER, ***Animal Liberation*** *(14 pp.)*

As a philosopher, ethicist, and animal rights activist, Singer argues for a change in attitude toward nonhumans as "utilities," especially as subjects for scientific experiments: "There is no characteristic that human infants possess that adult mammals do not have to the same or a higher degree."

Strategies: Definition, Classification/Division, Argument and Persuasion
Themes: Ethics/Values, Science

ADAM SMITH, ***Everyday Drugs*** *(2 pp.)*

Financial analyst Smith (George J. W. Goodman) challenges our idea of what constitutes a drug: "A coffee drinker who drinks coffee all day and cannot function without it is just a heavy coffee drinker, but someone using a non-okay drug is a 'drug user' or an addict."

Strategies: Comparison/Contrast, Definition, Satire
Theme: Popular Culture

SUSAN SONTAG, ***AIDS and Its Metaphors*** *(10 pp.)*

Writing in 1989, essayist, critic, and novelist Sontag anatomizes the metaphors through which AIDS is discussed—and misunderstood. "The plague metaphor is an essential vehicle of the most pessimistic reading of the epidemiological prospects. From classic fiction to the latest journalism, the standard plague story is of inexorability, inescapability."

Strategies: Comparison, Contrast, Definition, Classification/Division
Themes: Science, Language

SUSAN SONTAG, ***Beauty*** *(3 pp.)*

Writing for *Vogue* in 1975, critic and novelist Sontag argues that "the way women are taught to be involved with beauty encourages narcissism, reinforces dependence and immaturity."

Strategies: Comparison/Contrast, Definition, Argument and Persuasion
Themes: Ethics/Values, Gender, Language

GARY SOTO, ***The Grandfather*** *(3 pp.)*

Memoirist Soto interprets his Mexican American immigrant grandfather's life through the metaphor of his garden and especially of his favorite specimen, an avocado tree: "It grew, as did his family, and when he died, all his sons standing on each other's shoulders, oldest to youngest, could not reach the highest branches."

Strategies: Narration, Metaphor
Themes: Cultural Diversity, Family, Coming of Age

GARY SOTO, ***Like Mexicans*** *(4 pp.)*

Urged by his family to marry a Mexican girl, Soto surprises himself by falling in love with a Japanese woman. Meeting his future in-laws for the first time, Soto notes with relief that "these people are just like Mexicans. . . . Poor people. . . . like Mexicans, only different."

Strategies: Comparison/Contrast, Narration

Themes: Ethics/Values, Cultural Diversity, Family, Coming of Age

GARY SOTO, ***The Pie*** *(3 pp.)*

Mexican American memoirist Soto recollects himself as a boy "holy in almost every bone," yet guilty of a childhood sin committed in a moment of boredom: the theft of an apple pie which he devoured in one sitting. In this poignant story, Soto defines sin as "what you take and [don't] give back."

Strategies: Definition, Narration, Analogy

Themes: Ethics/Values, Family, Coming of Age

WILLIAM STAFFORD, ***A Way of Writing*** *(6 pp.)*

Stafford, a poet and writer, explains his thoughts on the writing process: "A writer . . . is someone who has found a process that will bring about new things he would not have thought of if he had not started to say them."

Strategies: Definition, Process Analysis

Themes: Writing, Work (and Play)

ELIZABETH CADY STANTON, ***Declaration of Sentiments and Resolutions*** *(5 pp.)*

Stanton, a leader of the American women's rights movement in the nineteenth century, modeled her "Declaration of Sentiments and Resolutions" (1848) on the Declaration of Independence: "We hold these truths to be self-evident: that all men and women are created equal."

Strategies: Analogy, Argument and Persuasion, Cause/Effect

Themes: Politics/Government, Human/Civil Rights, Gender

BRENT STAPLES, ***Black Men and Public Space*** *(4 pp.)*

New York Times editor Staples describes numerous encounters that led him to realize how as a black man he is stereotyped as dangerous: "At dark, shadowy intersections, I could cross in front of a car stopped at a traffic light and elicit the *thunk, thunk, thunk, thunk* of the driver . . . hammering down the door locks."

Strategies: Definition, Satire

Themes: Ethics/Values, Human/Civil Rights, Coming of Age

BRENT STAPLES, ***The "Scientific" War on the Poor*** *(3 pp.)*

Staples, a psychologist and journalist, explains how the misuse of I.Q. tests affected immigrants and the poor as a means of "quality control" during the early twentieth century. He argues that "a basic confusion between pseudoscience and the real thing" resulted in the deportation of "undesirable" white immigrants.

Strategies: Classification/Division, Argument and Persuasion, Cause/Effect
Themes: Ethics/Values, Human/Civil Rights, Science

SHELBY STEELE, ***On Being Black and Middle Class*** *(11 pp.)*

Steele uses this essay to illustrate the effects of a "pattern of racial identification . . . [that] asks us to see ourselves as an embattled minority, and . . . urges an adversarial stance toward the mainstream" and the divide between middle class and the lower class African Americans.

Strategies: Definition, Classification/Division, Cause/Effect
Themes: Human/Civil Rights, Community

SHELBY STEELE, ***The Recoloring of Campus Life*** *(13 pp.)*

Through interviews with a number of black and white students, social analyst and essayist Steele discovers a divisive "politics of difference" on college campuses: "When difference is the currency of power, each group must fight for the innocence that entitles it to power."

Strategies: Illustration, Argument and Persuasion, Cause/Effect
Themes: Politics/Government, Community, Education

SHELBY STEELE, ***White Guilt*** *(10 pp.)*

Steele here argues that lingering white guilt over discrimination against blacks—guilt many black leaders encourage—has had a profoundly negative effect on racial policy: "White guilt has pressured many of America's racial policies toward a paternalism that makes it difficult for blacks to find their true mettle or develop a faith in their own capacity to run as fast as others."

Strategies: Narration, Argument and Persuasion, Cause/Effect
Themes: Politics/Government, Human/Civil Rights, Education

GLORIA STEINEM, ***Why Young Women Are More Conservative*** *(8 pp.)*

Cofounder of *Ms.* magazine and feminist activist, Steinem explains why college women are more conservative than their male counterparts: These women, she argues, have not had the "radicalizing" experiences of "marrying and finding out that it is not yet an equal partnership; having children and discovering who is responsible for them and who is not; and aging, still a greater penalty for women than for men."

Strategies: Illustration, Classification/Division, Cause/Effect
Themes: Ethics/Values, Human/Civil Rights, Gender

JONATHAN SWIFT, ***A Modest Proposal*** *(8 pp.)*

In this most widely reprinted English essay of the eighteenth century, Swift satirizes brutal absentee English landlords for starving the Irish peasantry; if, in their greed, they are going to devour their poor tenants' resources, why not literally eat Irish children: "I have been assured by a very knowing American of my acquaintance in London, that a young healthy child well nursed is at a year old a most delicious, nourishing, and wholesome food, whether stewed, roasted, baked, or boiled."

Strategies: Satire, Argument and Persuasion, Cause/Effect, Process Analysis
Themes: Ethics/Values, Politics/Government, Family, Work

AMY TAN, ***The Language of Discretion*** *(9 pp.)*

As a writer closely connected to her Chinese heritage, Tan illustrates the misinterpretations that arise when linguistic differences between Chinese and English are compared "one-for-one." To understand meaning and intent, a "word-for-word translation is not enough."

Strategies: Comparison/Contrast, Definition, Process Analysis
Themes: Cultural Diversity, Language

AMY TAN, ***Mother Tongue*** *(6 pp.)*

At the core of Tan's writing is her fascination with the different "Englishes" she and her mother use in daily life and people's perceptions of them because of these differences: "Lately, I've been giving more thought to the kind of English my mother speaks. . . . 'broken' or 'fractured' English. But I wince when I say that."

Strategies: Comparison/Contrast, Narration
Themes: Cultural Diversity, Family, Language

AMY TAN, ***Snapshot: Lost Lives of Women*** *(4 pp.)*

In this essay, Tan examines a photograph taken in the 1920s of several generations of her female ancestors in China. Noting that it is an image of "secrets and tragedies," Tan also writes of the strength she found in these "women who never let [her] forget why stories need to be told."

Strategies: Comparison/Contrast, Narration, Analogy
Themes: Cultural Diversity, Writing, Communication, Gender

DEBORAH TANNEN, ***Communication Styles*** *(5 pp.)*

An expert on communication across cultural and gender lines, linguist Tannen argues that "the goal of complete equal opportunity in class may not be attainable, but realizing that one monolithic classroom-participation structure is not equal opportunity is itself a powerful motivation to find more diverse methods to serve diverse students."

Strategies: Comparison/Contrast, Argument and Persuasion, Cause/Effect
Themes: Gender, Language

DEBORAH TANNEN, ***Fast Forward: Technologically Enhanced Aggression (15 pp.)***

Tannen, a sociolinguist, here suggests that technological advances, particularly e-mail and other means of electronic communication via the Internet, make possible "not only new levels of connection but also new levels of hostility and enhanced means of expressing it."

Strategies: Argument and Persuasion, Cause/Effect
Themes: Popular Culture, Gender, Language

DEBORAH TANNEN, ***Sex, Lies, and Conversation (6 pp.)***

Tannen here contrasts the differing conversational styles of men and women, which often lead couples into misunderstanding and resentment. She suggests that "a sociolinguistic approach by which male-female conversation is seen as cross-cultural communication allows us to understand the problem and forge solutions without blaming either party."

Strategies: Comparison/Contrast, Illustration
Themes: Gender, Language

PAUL THEROUX, ***Being a Man (4 pp.)***

Critic Theroux is here uncharacteristically serious and straightforward in his objections to the stereotypes of manliness: "Even the expression 'Be a man!' strikes me as insulting and abusive. It means: Be stupid, be unfeeling, obedient, soldierly, and stop thinking."

Strategies: Comparison/Contrast, Definition, Description
Themes: Ethics/Values, Popular Culture, Gender

PHYLLIS THEROUX, ***My Father, the Prince (4 pp.)***

Theroux, a journalist and autobiographer, writes to reinforce fathers' crucial importance in their daughters' lives, focusing particularly on her own father's inspiring ability to impart "the promise that ahead of me was dry land—a bright, marshless territory, without chuckholes or traps, where one day I would walk easily."

Strategies: Description, Narration, Metaphor
Themes: Family, Coming of Age, Work (and Play)

LEWIS THOMAS, ***Notes on Punctuation*** *(3 pp.)*

Physician and essayist Thomas provides some whimsical advice for using common punctuation marks. For example, "with a semicolon there you get a pleasant little feeling of expectancy; there is more to come; read on; it will get clearer."

Strategies: Illustration, Classification/Division
Theme: Writing

LEWIS THOMAS, ***On Magic in Medicine*** *(5 pp.)*

Thomas, a physician and essayist, warns against accepting simple solutions for staying healthy. The problem, in his view, is that "it is much more difficult to be convincing about ignorance concerning disease mechanisms than it is to make claims for full comprehension, especially when the comprehension leads, logically or not, to some sort of action."

Strategies: Illustration, Cause/Effect
Themes: Ethics/Values

LEWIS THOMAS, ***On Natural Death*** *(3 pp.)*

Thomas, a physician and writer, offers a sensitive but matter-of-fact meditation on the end of life, providing biological evidence that most deaths are painless: "Pain is useful for avoidance, for getting away when there's time to get away, but when it is end game, and no way back, pain is likely to be turned off, and the mechanisms for this are wonderfully precise and quick."

Strategies: Illustration, Argument and Persuasion, Process Analysis
Themes: Ethics/Values, Nature

HENRY DAVID THOREAU, ***The Battle of the Ants*** *(3 pp.)*

As nineteenth-century naturalist Thoreau witnesses an epic battle between red and black ants in territorial combat, the struggle takes on almost historic proportions: "And certainly there is not the fight recorded in Concord history, at least, if in the history of America, that will bear a moment's comparison with this, whether for the numbers engaged in it, or for the patriotism and heroism displayed."

Strategies: Narration, Classification, Analogy
Theme: Nature

HENRY DAVID THOREAU, ***Civil Disobedience*** *(18 pp.)*

An ardent abolitionist and opponent of the Mexican War, Thoreau protested government policies and was jailed for not paying taxes, writing, "If a thousand men were not to pay their tax-bills this year, that would not be a violent and bloody measure, as it would be to pay them, and enable the State to commit violence and shed innocent blood. This is, in fact, the definition of a peaceable revolution."

Strategies: Illustration, Classification/Division, Argument and Persuasion
Themes: Ethics/Values, Politics/Government, Human/Civil Rights

HENRY DAVID THOREAU, ***Where I Lived, and What I Lived For*** *(6 pp.)*

In the guise of a rustic philosopher, Thoreau offers a philosophical manifesto and meditation on nature and what is—and is not—essential to a life well lived: "I went to the woods because I wished to live deliberately, to front only the essential facts of life, and see if I could not learn what it had to teach, and not, when I came to die, discover that I had not lived."

Strategies: Illustration, Narration, Metaphor, Argument and Persuasion
Themes: Ethics/Values, nature, Coming of Age

JAMES THURBER, ***The Bear Who Let It Alone*** *(2 pp.)*

Thurber's fable of the mead-swilling bear whose rambunctious behavior didn't change even after he became "a famous teetotaler" ends with the moral "*You might as well fall flat on your face as lean over too far backward.*"

Strategies: Narration, Metaphor, Argument and Persuasion
Themes: Ethics/Values, Nature, Coming of Age

JAMES THURBER, ***University Days*** *(6 pp.)*

In this all-time favorite, Thurber caricatures students and faculty alike, illustrating various perennial student ineptitudes, mostly his own: athletic (he can't pass gym except by cheating); military drill ("having failed military . . . I was the only senior still in uniform"); and academic: "'That's your eye!'" shouted the botany professor. "'You've fixed the [microscope] lens so that it reflects! You've drawn your eye!'"

Strategies: Illustration, Narration, Classification/Division
Themes: Ethics/Values, Coming of Age, Work (and Play), Education

SALLIE TISDALE, ***We Do Abortions Here: A Nurse's Story*** *(8 pp.)*

A former abortion clinic nurse, freelance writer Tisdale offers graphic descriptions of her experiences: "I look at abortion as if I am standing on a cliff with a telescope, gazing at some great vista. I can sweep the horizon with both eyes, survey the scene in all its distance and size. Or I can put my eye to the lens and focus on the small details, suddenly so close."

Strategies: Description, Illustration, Process Analysis

Themes: Ethics/Values, Family, Gender

SUSAN ALLEN TOTH, ***Boyfriends** (6 pp.)*

Autobiographer Toth uses her relationship with her first boyfriend in Iowa to represent the typical pattern of high school courtship in the 1950s: "meticulously slow, progressing through inquiry, phone calls, planned encounters in public places, double or triple dates, single dates, handholding, and finally a good-night kiss."

Strategies: Illustration, Narration, Process Analysis

Themes: Family, Coming of Age, Work (and Play), Gender

CALVIN TRILLIN, ***It's Just Too Late** (10 pp.)*

Trillin tells the complicated story of the brief life and abrupt death of teenager FaNee Cooper, who in the 1970s drifted into drinking, drugs, and a circle of "freak" friends: "She was thought to be not just super-intelligent but super-mysterious, and even, at times, super-weird—an introverted girl who stared straight ahead with deep-brown, nearly black eyes and seemed to have thoughts she couldn't share."

Strategies: Comparison/Contrast, Narration, Process Analysis

Themes: Ethics/Values, Human/Civil Rights, Family, Work (and Play)

BARBARA TUCHMAN, ***"This Is the End of the World": The Black Death** (11 pp.)*

Tuchman, a Pulitzer Prize-winning historian, describes the spread of bubonic plague during the fourteenth century: "In the countryside peasants dropped dead on the roads, in the fields, in their houses. Survivors in growing helplessness fell into apathy, leaving ripe wheat uncut and livestock untended."

Strategies: Narration, Analogy, Metaphor, Cause/Effect

Themes: Ethics/Values, Community

MARK TWAIN, ***Uncle John's Farm** (7 pp.)*

Nineteenth-century novelist Twain recreates, with his customary wit, happy childhood visits to his uncle's farm, relishing sensory details but also more furtive pleasures: "Down a piece . . . a limpid brook . . . sang along over its gravelly bed and curved and frisked in and out and here and there and yonder in the deep shade of overhanging foliage and vines—a divine place for wading, and it had swimming pools, too, which were forbidden to us and therefore much frequented by us."

Strategies: Illustration, Narration, Classification/Division

Themes: Ethics/Values, Coming of Age, Work (and Play), Education

JOHN UPDIKE, ***The Disposable Rocket*** *(4 pp.)*

A noted novelist, poet, and essayist, Updike marvels at the male and female reproductive systems: "From the standpoint of reproduction, the male body is a delivery system, as the female is a mazy device for retention."

Strategies: Comparison/Contrast, Description, Metaphor

Themes: Nature, Gender

GORE VIDAL, ***Drugs*** *(3 pp.)*

In this 1970 essay, novelist Vidal claims that the way to stop drug abuse in the United States is to "simply make all drugs available and sell them at cost" so there will be "no money in it for anyone."

Strategies: Narration, Argument and Persuasion, Cause/Effect

Themes: Ethics/Values, Popular Culture

JUDITH VIORST, ***Friends, Good Friends—And Such Good Friends*** *(5 pp.)*

Viorst, a poet and journalist, classifies eight types of women's friendship, noting that "the friendships I have and the friendships I see are conducted at many levels of intensity, serve many different functions, meet different needs, and range from those as all-the-way as the friendship of the soul sisters to that of the most nonchalant and casual playmates."

Strategies: Definition, Illustration, Classification/Division

Themes: Community, Gender

KURT VONNEGUT, ***How to Write with Style*** *(4 pp.)*

Vonnegut, a novelist, offers eight practical suggestions to help writers express themselves with clarity, precision, economy, and in their own voice: "If you scribble your thoughts any which way, your readers will surely feel that you care nothing about them. They will mark you down as an egomaniac or a chowderhead—or worse, they will stop reading you."

Strategy: Process Analysis

Theme: Writing

ALICE WALKER, ***Beauty: When the Other Dancer Is the Self*** *(8 pp.)*

Poet, essayist, and novelist Walker here reflects on a childhood injury that blinded her in one eye; even after the "glob of whitish scar tissue" was surgically removed, Walker felt disfigured. When her young daughter, recalling a picture of the earth encircled by clouds, says, "Mommy, there's a *world* in your eye," Walker finally feels "beautiful, whole and free."

Strategies: Narration, Metaphor

Themes: Ethics/Values, Family, Coming of Age

ALICE WALKER, ***In Search of Our Mothers' Gardens*** *(9 pp.)*

Pulitzer Prize-winning novelist Walker considers the plight of generations of poor African American women "driven to a numb and bleeding madness by the springs of creativity in them for which there was no release."

Strategies: Definition, Illustration, Cause/Effect

Themes: Human/Civil Rights, Family, Gender

EUDORA WELTY, ***Eavesdropping*** *(3 pp.)*

"Ever since I was first read to," by loving parents and teachers, says Pulitzer Prize-winning novelist and short-story writer Welty, "then started reading to myself, there has never been a line read that I didn't *hear*."

Strategies: Definition, Description, Narration

Themes: Family, Popular Culture, Coming of Age, Education

E. B. WHITE, ***Once More to the Lake*** *(6 pp.)*

Returning with his son to the Maine lake where he summered as a child, White ponders how little things have changed there and reflects poignantly on how the cycles of life repeat themselves: "I would be in the middle of some simple act, I would be picking up a bait box or laying down a table fork, or I would be saying something, and suddenly it would be not I but my father who was saying the words or making the gesture."

Strategies: Comparison/Contrast, Illustration, Narration

Themes: Ethics/Values, Family, Coming of Age, Work (and Play)

E. B. WHITE, ***The Ring of Time*** *(4 pp.)*

Witnessing a young circus rider as she practices her routine circling a big-top ring on horseback, White finds a moment of perfection when time gives the illusion of standing still: "Everything in her movements, her expression, told you that for her the ring of time was perfectly formed, changeless, predictable, without beginning or end, like the ring in which she was travelling at this moment with the horse that wallowed under her."

Strategies: Comparison/Contrast, Illustration, Narration
Themes: Ethics/Values, Family, Coming of Age, Work (and Play)

BARBARA DAFOE WHITEHEAD, ***Where Have All the Parents Gone?*** *(7 pp.)*

Social historian Whitehead critiques public policies based on "investing in kids" at the expense of providing support for parents. "For proponents of the *kids as capital* argument, the logic is clear: why try to help parents—an increasingly marginal and unsympathetic bunch—when you can rescue their children?"

Strategies: Definition, Argument and Persuasion
Themes: Politics/Government, Family, Community, Work (and Play)

GEORGE WILL, ***Our Schools for Scandal*** *(3 pp.)*

Will, a syndicated columnist, argues that the exploitation of college athletes is a scandal that "involves slipping academically unqualified young men in the back doors of academic institutions, insulating them from academic expectations, wringing them dry of their athletic-commercial usefulness, then slinging them out the back door even less suited to society than they were when they entered."

Strategies: Illustration, Argument and Persuasion
Themes: Popular Culture, Work (and Play), Education

PATRICIA J. WILLIAMS, ***The Death of the Profane*** *(7 pp.)*

Barred from a clothing store because of her race, Williams, a law professor, tried to explain her experience and her sense of rage in an article for a law review. Discovering in the edited version that her "fury had been carefully cut out . . ." as a "'matter of style,'" she focuses "on the law-review editing process as a consequence of an ideology of style rooted in a social text of neutrality."

Strategies: Description, Narration, Argument and Persuasion
Themes: Ethics/Values, Human/Civil Rights, Writing

TERRY TEMPEST WILLIAMS, ***The Clan of One-Breasted Women*** *(7 pp.)*

Environmentalist Williams blames nuclear testing in the Utah deserts during the 1950s and 1960s for the unusually high rate of cancer in her family: "My mother, my grandmothers, and six aunts have all had mastectomies. Seven are dead."

Strategies: Argument and Persuasion, Cause/Effect
Themes: Ethics/Values, Politics/Government, Science, Environment, Family

MARIE WINN, ***Family Life* (10 *pp.*)**

Television, argues Winn, a cultural critic, has greatly diminished the quality of American family life: "In its effect on family relationships, in its facilitation of parental withdrawal from an active role in the socialization of their children, and in its replacement of family rituals and special events, television has played an important role in the disintegration of the American family."

Strategies: Classification/Division, Argument and Persuasion, Cause/Effect

Themes: Family, Work (and Play)

TOM WOLFE, ***The Right Stuff* (4 *pp.*)**

In this excerpt from Wolfe's book about the U. S. space program's early days, he celebrates the death-defying courage that allows a fighter pilot "to go up in a hurtling piece of machinery and put his hide on the line and then have the moxie, the reflexes, the experience, the coolness, to pull it back in the last yawning moment."

Strategies: Definition, Description, Narration

Themes: Ethics/Values

ELIZABETH WONG, ***The Struggle to Be an All-American Girl* (3 *pp.*)**

Wong, a journalist and playwright, describes how as a child she resisted learning Chinese, the language of her immigrant parents: "I thought of myself as multicultural. I preferred tacos to egg rolls; I enjoyed Cinco de Mayo more than Chinese New Year."

Strategies: Illustration, Narration

Themes: Cultural Diversity, Coming of Age, Education

VIRGINIA WOOLF, ***The Death of the Moth* (3 *pp.*)**

In this reverie, novelist and essayist Woolf minutely examines a moth fluttering around a windowpane until, its energy expended, it dies: "O yes, he seemed to say, death is stronger than I am."

Strategies: Description, Analogy, Metaphor

Themes: Nature, Ethics/Values

VIRGINIA WOOLF, ***Shakespeare's Sister* (12 *pp.*)**

In contemplating why history has produced so few women writers, Woolf imagines that Shakespeare had a sister whose literary genius matched his, but whose literary expression was stifled by conventional mores: "Any woman born with a great gift in the sixteenth century . . . would have been so thwarted and hindered by other people, so tortured and pulled asunder by her own contrary instincts, that she must have lost her health and sanity to a certainty."

Strategies: Comparison/Contrast, Argument and Persuasion, Cause/Effect
Themes: Writing, Gender

RICHARD WRIGHT, ***The Power of Books*** **(9 *pp.*)**

In this chapter from his autobiography, Wright describes how he faced down the many obstacles blocking a black man of his day from reading and developed a passion for books that would lead him to become a writer himself: "Occasionally, for a few days, I would stop reading. But a vague hunger would come over me for books, books that opened up new avenues of feeling and seeing, and again I would forge another note to the white librarian."

Strategies: Illustration, Narration, Process Analysis
Themes: Human/Civil Rights, Writing, Coming of Age

WILLIAM ZINSSER, ***Clutter*** **(5 *pp.*)**

Journalist and writing teacher Zinsser offers advice on how to "simplify, simplify": "Writing improves in direct ratio to the number of things we can keep out of it that shouldn't be there."

Strategies: Description, Illustration, Argument and Persuasion
Theme: Writing

THE RHETORICAL TABLE OF CONTENTS FOR *THE ST. MARTIN'S CUSTOM READER*

ANALOGY

ARGUMENT AND PERSUASION

CAUSE/EFFECT

CLASSIFICATION/DIVISION

COMPARISON/CONTRAST

DEFINITION

DESCRIPTION

ILLUSTRATION

METAPHOR

NARRATION

PROCESS ANALYSIS

SATIRE

THE THEMATIC TABLE OF CONTENTS FOR *THE ST. MARTIN'S CUSTOM READER*

COMING OF AGE

COMMUNITY

CULTURAL DIVERSITY

EDUCATION

CURTIS CHANG, ***Streets of Gold: The Myth of the Model Minority*** (10 pp.)

AARON COPLAND, ***How We Listen to Music*** (6 pp.)

RALPH WALDO EMERSON, ***The American Scholar*** (14 pp.)

FRANCES FITZGERALD, ***Rewriting American History*** (7 pp.)

PAUL FUSSELL, ***The Boy Scout Handbook*** (5 pp.)

HENRY LOUIS GATES JR., ***The Debate Has Been Miscast from the Start*** (5 pp.)

HENRY LOUIS GATES JR., ***Talking Black*** (9 pp.)

NATHAN GLAZER, ***Some Very Modest Proposals for the Improvement of American Education*** (7 pp.)

DONALD HALL, ***Four Ways of Reading*** (4 pp.)

S. I. HAYAKAWA, ***How Dictionaries Are Made*** (3 pp.)

NAT HENTOFF, ***Free Speech on Campus*** (6 pp.)

JOHN HOLT, ***How Teachers Make Children Hate Reading*** (8 pp.)

PERRI KLASS, ***Learning the Language*** (4 pp.)

JONATHAN KOZOL, ***The Human Cost of an Illiterate Society*** (pp.8)

MALCOLM X, ***Coming to an Awareness of Language*** (3 pp.)

MARY E. MEBANE, ***Shades of Black*** (5 pp.)

CASEY MILLER AND KATE SWIFT, ***Who's in Charge of the English Language?*** (7 pp.)

DONALD M. MURRAY, ***The Maker's Eye: Revising Your Own Manuscripts*** (9 pp.)

WILLIAM RASPBERRY, ***The Handicap of Definition*** (3 pp.)

PAUL ROBERTS, ***How to Say Nothing in Five Hundred Words*** (12 pp.)

RICHARD RODRIGUEZ, ***Aria: A Memoir of a Bilingual Childhood*** (12 pp.)

RICHARD RODRIGUEZ, ***None of This Is Fair*** (5 pp.)

MIKE ROSE, ***"I Just Wanna Be Average"*** (8 pp.)

SHELBY STEELE, ***The Recoloring of Campus Life*** (13 pp.)

SHELBY STEELE, ***White Guilt*** (10 pp.)

JAMES THURBER, ***University Days*** (6 pp.)

MARK TWAIN, ***Uncle John's Farm*** (7 pp.)

EUDORA WELTY, ***Eavesdropping*** (3 pp.)

GEORGE WILL, ***Our Schools for Scandal*** (3 pp.)

ELIZABETH WONG, ***The Struggle to Be an All-American Girl*** (3 pp.)

ENVIRONMENT

ETHICS/VALUES

FAMILY

GENDER

HUMAN/CIVIL RIGHTS

LANGUAGE

NATURE

PLACES

POLITICS/GOVERNMENT

POPULAR CULTURE

SCIENCE

WORK (AND PLAY)

WRITING

THREE SAMPLE READINGS FROM *THE ST. MARTIN'S CUSTOM READER*

ZORA NEALE HURSTON

How It Feels to Be Colored Me

Folklorist and writer Zora Neale Hurston (1903–1960) was born in Eatonville, Florida, a self-governing all-black town, and graduated from Barnard College (B.A., 1928). Hurston's work with anthropologist Frank Boaz gave her a perspective, "the spyglass of anthropology," through which to study African American folklore. Her *Mules and Men* (1935) celebrates African American culture by presenting jokes, myths, and stories in vernacular Black English. Hurston also published an autobiography, *Dust Tracks on a Road* (1942). Although she was an important figure in the Harlem Renaissance arts movement of the 1920s and 1930s, Hurston's contemporaries criticized her for refusing to take up political protest and for creating stereotypically "primitive" characters in her novels. Richard Wright, for example, said that her novel *Their Eyes Were Watching God* (1937) "carries no theme, no message, no thought." Contemporary critic Mary Helen Washington, on the other hand, extols the novel for its "powerful, articulate, self-reliant, and radically different" black heroine. Although her work was neglected until recently, interest in her writing has grown since it was revived by Alice Walker, who wrote in *Ms.* (1975) of her quest to find, and place a marker on, Hurston's grave. In the autobiographical essay "How It Feels to Be Colored Me" (1928), from the first anthology of Hurston's work, *I Love Myself When I'm Laughing*... (1979), edited by Alice Walker, Hurston reports on the triumph of her exuberant spirit over any suggestion of racial inferiority.

I am colored but I offer nothing in the way of extenuating circumstances except the fact that I am the only Negro in the United States whose grandfather on the mother's side was *not* an Indian chief.

I remember the very day that I became colored. Up to my thirteenth year I lived in the little Negro town of Eatonville, Florida. It is exclusively a colored town. The only white people I knew passed through the town going to or coming from Orlando. The native whites rode dusty horses, the Northern tourists chugged down the sandy village road in automobiles. The town knew the Southerners and never stopped cane chewing when they passed. But the Northerners were something else again. They were peered at cautiously from behind curtains by the timid. The more venturesome would come out on the porch to watch them go past and got just as much pleasure out of the tourists as the tourists got out of the village.

The front porch might seem a daring place for the rest of the town, but it was a gallery seat for me. My favorite place was atop the gate-post. Proscenium box for a born first-nighter. Not only did I enjoy the show, but I didn't mind the actors knowing that I liked it. I usually spoke to them in passing. I'd wave at them and when they returned my salute, I would say something like this: "Howdy-do-well-I-thank-you-where-you-goin'?" Usually automobile or the horse paused at this, and after a queer exchange of compliments, I would probably "go a piece of the way" with them, as we say in farthest Florida. If one of my family happened to come to the front in time to see me, of course negotiations would be rudely broken off. But even so, it is clear that I was the first "welcome-to-our-state" Floridian, and I hope the Miami Chamber of Commerce will please take notice.

During this period, white people differed from colored to me only in that they rode through town and never lived there. They liked to hear me "speak pieces" and sing and wanted to see me dance the parse-me-la, and gave me generously of their small silver for doing these things, which seemed strange to me for I wanted to do them so much that I needed bribing to stop. Only they didn't know it. The colored people gave no dimes. They deplored any joyful tendencies in me, but I was their Zora nevertheless. I belonged to them, to the nearby hotels, to the county—everybody's Zora.

But changes came in the family when I was thirteen, and I was sent 5
to school in Jacksonville. I left Eatonville, the town of the oleanders, as Zora. When I disembarked from the river-boat at Jacksonville, she was no more. It seemed that I had suffered a sea change. I was not Zora of Orange County any more, I was now a little colored girl. I found it out in certain ways. In my heart as well as in the mirror, I became a fast brown—warranted not to rub nor run.

But I am not tragically colored. There is no great sorrow dammed up in my soul, nor lurking behind my eyes. I do not mind at all. I do not belong to the sobbing school of Negrohood who hold that nature somehow has given them a lowdown dirty deal and whose feelings are all hurt about it. Even in the helter-skelter skirmish that is my life, I have seen that the world is to the strong regardless of a little pigmentation more or less. No, I do not weep at the world—I am too busy sharpening my oyster knife.

Someone is always at my elbow reminding me that I am the granddaughter of slaves. It fails to register depression with me. Slavery is sixty years in the past. The operation was successful and the patient is doing well, thank you. The terrible struggle that made me an American out of a potential slave said “On the line!” The Reconstruction said “Get set!”; and the generation before said “Go!” I am off to a flying start and I must not halt in the stretch to look behind and weep. Slavery is the price I paid for civilization, and the choice was not with me. It is a bully adventure and worth all that I have paid through my ancestors for it. No one on earth ever had a greater chance for glory. The world to be won and nothing to be lost. It is thrilling to think—to know that for any act of mine, I shall get twice as much praise or twice as much blame. It is quite exciting to hold the center of the national stage, with the spectators not knowing whether to laugh or to weep.

The position of my white neighbors is much more difficult. No brown specter pulls up a chair beside me when I sit down to eat. No dark ghost thrusts its leg against mine in bed. The game of keeping what one has is never so exciting as the game of getting.

I do not always feel colored. Even now I often achieve the unconscious Zora of Eatonville before the Hegira. I feel most colored when I am thrown against a sharp white background.

For instance at Barnard, “Beside the waters of the Hudson” I feel my 10
race. Among the thousand white persons, I am a dark rock surged upon, and overswept, but through it all, I remain myself. When covered by the waters, I am; and the ebb but reveals me again.

Sometimes it is the other way around. A white person is set down in our midst, but the contrast is just as sharp for me. For instance, when I sit in the drafty basement that is The New World Cabaret with a white person, my color comes. We enter chatting about any little nothing that we have in common and are seated by the jazz waiters. In the abrupt way that jazz orchestras have, this one plunges into a number. It loses no time in circumlocutions, but gets right down to business. It constricts the thorax and splits the heart with its tempo and narcotic harmonies. This orchestra grows rambunctious, rears on its hind legs and attacks the tonal veil with primitive fury, rending it, clawing it until it breaks through to the jungle beyond. I follow those heathen—follow them exultingly. I dance wildly inside myself; I yell within, I whoop; I shake my assegai above my head, I hurl it true to the mark *yeeeeooww!* I am in the jungle and living in the jungle way. My face is painted red and yellow and my body is painted blue. My pulse is throbbing like a war drum. I want to slaughter something—give pain, give death to what, I do not know. But the piece ends. The men of the orchestra wipe their lips and rest their fingers. I creep back slowly to the veneer we call civilization with the last tone and find the white friend sitting motionless in his seat, smoking calmly.

"Good music they have here," he remarks, drumming the table with his fingertips.

Music. The great blobs of purple and red emotion have not touched him. He has only heard what I felt. He is far away and I see him but dimly across the ocean and the continent that have fallen between us. He is so pale with his whiteness then and I am *so* colored.

At certain times I have no race, I am *me.* When I set my hat at a certain angle and saunter down Seventh Avenue, Harlem City, feeling as snooty as the lions in front of the Forty-Second Street Library, for instance. So far as my feelings are concerned, Peggy Hopkins Joyce on the Boule Mich with her gorgeous raiment, stately carriage, knees knocking together in a most aristocratic manner, has nothing on me. The cosmic Zora emerges. I belong to no race nor time. I am the eternal feminine with its string of beads.

15 I have no separate feeling about being an American citizen and colored. I am merely a fragment of the Great Soul that surges within the boundaries. My country, right or wrong.

Sometimes, I feel discriminated against, but it does not make me angry. It merely astonishes me. How *can* any deny themselves the pleasure of my company? It's beyond me.

But in the main, I feel like a brown bag of miscellany propped against a wall. Against a wall in company with other bags, white, red, and yellow. Pour out the contents, and there is discovered a jumble of small things priceless and worthless. A first-water diamond, an empty spool, bits of broken glass, lengths of string, a key to a door long since crumbled away, a rusty knife-blade, old shoes saved for a road that never was and never will be, a nail bent under the weight of things too heavy for any nail, a dried flower or two still a little fragrant. In your hand is the brown bag. On the ground before you is the jumble it held—so much like the jumble in the bags, could they be emptied, that all might be dumped in a single heap and the bags refilled without altering the content of any greatly. A bit of colored glass more or less would not matter. Perhaps that is how the Great Stuffer of Bags filled them in the first place—who knows?

THOMAS JEFFERSON

The Declaration of Independence

Thomas Jefferson (1743–1826), of Charlottesville, Virginia, was—like his fellow patriot Benjamin Franklin—a renaissance man. Educated at the College of William and Mary, later the founder of the University of Virginia, Jefferson excelled as a philosopher, architect, inventor, writer, and, above all, a consummate politician. A patrician and revolutionary who embodied the democratic spirit of the new nation, Jefferson served as a delegate to the Continental Congress in 1775, as governor of the Commonwealth of Virginia, and as third president of the United States. With Franklin and John Adams, Jefferson drafted America's most incendiary document, the Declaration of Independence, in mid-June 1776. Revised by the Continental Congress, it was signed on July 4. The Declaration, often called "an expression of the American mind," reflects Jefferson's belief that democracy is the ideal form of government, a philosophy reinforced in his refusal to sign the Constitution until the Bill of Rights was added. The Declaration is a deductive argument, based on the premise "We hold these truths to be self-evident," from which the rest of the argument follows. As events were to prove, what the colonists considered an emphatic, plainspoken statement of natural rights the British considered an inflammatory declaration of war.

IN CONGRESS, JULY 4, 1776
THE UNANIMOUS DECLARATION OF THE
THIRTEEN UNITED STATES OF AMERICA

When in the Course of human events it becomes necessary for one people to dissolve the political bands which have connected them with another, and to assume among the powers of the earth, the separate and equal station to which the Laws of Nature and of Nature's God entitle them, a decent respect to the opinions of mankind requires that they should declare the causes which impel them to the separation.

We hold these truths to be self-evident, that all men are created equal, that they are endowed by their Creator with certain unalienable Rights, that among these are Life, Liberty, and the pursuit of Happiness. That to secure these rights, Governments are instituted among Men, deriving their just powers from the consent of the governed. That whenever any Form of Government becomes destructive of these ends, it is the Right of the People to alter or to abolish it, and to institute new Government, laying its foundation on such principles and organizing its powers in such form, as to them shall seem most likely to effect their Safety and Happiness. Prudence, indeed, will dictate that Governments long established should not be changed for light and transient causes; and accordingly all experience hath shewn, that mankind are more disposed to suffer, while evils are sufferable, than to right themselves by abolishing the forms to which they are accustomed. But when a long train of abuses and usurpations, pursuing invariably the same Object evinces a design to reduce them under absolute Despotism, it is their right, it is their duty, to throw off such Government, and to provide new Guards for their future security. Such has been the patient sufferance of these Colonies; and such is now the necessity which constrains them to alter their former Systems of Government. The history of the present King of Great Britain is a history of repeated injuries and usurpations, all having in direct object the establishment of an absolute Tyranny over these States. To prove this, let Facts be submitted to a candid world.

He has refused his Assent to Laws, the most wholesome and necessary for the public good.

He has forbidden his Government to pass laws of immediate and pressing importance, unless suspended in their operation till his Assent should be obtained; and when so suspended, he has utterly neglected to attend to them.

He has refused to pass other Laws for the accommodation of large 5
districts of people, unless those people would relinquish the right of Representation in the Legislature, a right inestimable to them and formidable to tyrants only.

He has called together legislative bodies at places unusual, uncomfortable, and distant from the depository of their Public Records, for the sole purpose of fatiguing them into compliance with his measures.

He has dissolved Representative Houses repeatedly, for opposing with manly firmness his invasions on the rights of the people.

He has refused for a long time, after such dissolutions, to cause others to be elected; whereby the Legislative Powers, incapable of Annihilation, have returned to the People at large for their exercise; the State remaining in the mean time exposed to all the dangers of invasion from without, and convulsions within.

He has endeavoured to prevent the population of these States; for that purpose obstructing the Laws for Naturalization of Foreigners; refusing to pass others to encourage their migration hither, and raising the conditions of new Appropriations of Lands.

He has obstructed the Administration of Justice, by refusing his Assent to Laws for establishing Judiciary Powers.

He has made Judges dependent on his Will alone, for the tenure of their offices, and the amount and payment of their salaries.

He has erected a multitude of New Offices, and sent hither swarms of Officers to harass our People, and eat out their substance.

He has kept among us, in times of peace, Standing Armies without the Consent of our legislatures.

He has affected to render the Military independent of and superior to the Civil Power.

He has combined with others to subject us to a jurisdiction foreign to our constitution, and unacknowledged by our laws; giving his Assent to their Acts of pretended Legislation: For quartering large bodies of armed troops among us: For protecting them, by a mock Trial, from punishment for any Murders which they should commit on the Inhabitants of these States: For cutting off our Trade with all parts of the world: For imposing Taxes on us without our Consent: For depriving us in many cases, of the benefits of Trial by Jury; For transporting us beyond Seas to be tried for pretended offenses: for abolishing the free System of English Laws in a neighboring Province, establishing therein an Arbitrary government, and enlarging its Boundaries so as to render it at once an example and fit instrument for introducing the same absolute rule into these Colonies: For taking away our Charters, abolishing our most valuable Laws and altering fundamentally the Forms of our Governments: For suspending our own Legislatures, and declaring themselves invested with power to legislate for us in all cases whatsoever.

He has abdicated Government here, by declaring us out of his Protection and waging War against us.

He has plundered our seas, ravaged our Coasts, burnt our towns, and destroyed the lives of our people.

He is at this time transporting large Armies of foreign Mercenaries to complete the works of death, desolation and tyranny, already begun with circumstances of Cruelty & Perfidy scarcely paralleled in the most barbarous ages, and totally unworthy the Head of a civilized nation.

He has constrained our fellow Citizens taken Captive on the high Seas to bear Arms against their Country, to become the executioners of their friends and Brethren, or to fall themselves by their Hands.

He has excited domestic insurrections amongst us, and has endeavoured to bring on the inhabitants of our frontiers, the merciless Indian

Savages, whose known rule of warfare, is an undistinguished destruction of all ages, sexes, and conditions.

In every stage of these Oppressions We have Petitioned for Redress in the most humble terms: Our repeated Petitions have been answered only by repeated injury. A Prince, whose character is thus marked by every act which may define a Tyrant, is unfit to be the ruler of a free People.

Nor have We been wanting in attention to our British brethren. We have warned them from time to time of attempts by their legislature to extend an unwarrantable jurisdiction over us. We have reminded them of the circumstances of our emigration and settlement here. We have appealed to their native justice and magnanimity, and we have conjured them by the ties of our common kindred to disavow these usurpations, which would inevitably interrupt our connections and correspondence. They too have been deaf to the voice of justice and of consanguinity. We must, therefore, acquiesce in the necessity, which denounces our Separation, and hold them, as we hold the rest of mankind, Enemies in War, in Peace Friends.

We, THEREFORE the Representatives of the UNITED STATES OF AMERICA, in General Congress, Assembled, appealing to the Supreme Judge of the world for the rectitude of our intentions, do, in the Name, and by Authority of the good People of these Colonies, solemnly publish and declare, That these United Colonies are, and of Right ought to be FREE AND INDEPENDENT STATES; that they are Absolved from all Allegiance to the British Crown, and that all political connection between them and the State of Great Britain, is and ought to be totally dissolved; and that as Free and Independent States, they have full Power to levy War, conclude Peace, contract Alliances, establish Commerce, and to do all other Acts and Things which Independent States may of right do. And for the support of this Declaration, with a firm reliance on the protection of Divine Providence, we mutually pledge to each other our Lives, our Fortunes, and our sacred Honor.

ABRAHAM LINCOLN

The Gettysburg Address

The self-made, self-taught son of Kentucky pioneers, Abraham Lincoln (1809–1865) served four terms in the Illinois state legislature before being elected to Congress in 1847. As sixteenth president of the United States (1861–1865), Lincoln's supreme efforts were devoted to trying to secure the passage of the Thirteenth Amendment that would forever outlaw slavery, while preserving the Union amidst the bloody Civil War that threatened to destroy its young men, its economy, and the very government itself. Lincoln was a gifted writer of speeches at a time when public officials still wrote their own; his First and Second Inaugural Addresses join the Gettysburg Address as American classics. At the dedication of the battlefield at Gettysburg as a memorial to the thousands killed in the Civil War, however, Lincoln's delivery did not match his magnificent words. Lincoln was incubating smallpox ("At last I have something I can give to everybody," he joked) when he delivered the address "in a thin, high voice" that left his audience—accustomed to a booming oratory—unimpressed. The words, however, rich with biblical similes, birth metaphors, antitheses (oppositions and contrasts), and tricolons (the division of an idea into three harmonious parts—"government of the people, by the people, for the people"), still resonate today, simultaneously plainspoken and majestic.

Four score and seven years ago our fathers brought forth on this continent a new nation, conceived in liberty, and dedicated to the proposition that all men are created equal.

Now we are engaged in a great civil war, testing whether that nation, or any nation so conceived and so dedicated, can long endure. We are met on a great battlefield of that war. We have come to dedicate a portion of that field, as a final resting place for those who here gave their lives that the nation might live. It is altogether fitting and proper that we should do this.

But, in a larger sense, we cannot dedicate—we cannot consecrate—we cannot hallow—this ground. The brave men, living and dead, who struggled here, have consecrated it, far above our poor power to add or detract. The world will little note, nor long remember what we say here, but it can never forget what they did here. It is for us the living, rather, to be dedicated here to the unfinished work which they who fought here have thus far so nobly advanced. It is rather for us to be here dedicated to the great task remaining before us—that from these honored dead we take increased devotion—that we here highly resolve that these dead shall not have died in vain—that this nation, under God, shall have a new birth of freedom—and that the government of the people, by the people, for the people, shall not perish from the earth.

CREATING YOUR *ST. MARTIN'S CUSTOM READER* IN FOUR SIMPLE STEPS

1. **Get started online** The contents of this booklet mirror our Web site, http://customreader.bedfordstmartins.com, including an annotated table of contents, which provides a brief description of each reading, and alternate rhetorical and thematic listings. Use these tables of contents to generate ideas for possible selections to include in your reader.

2. **Preview the selections** To preview the full text of a selection, simply insert *The St. Martin's Custom Reader* CD-ROM into your computer's CD-ROM drive. While on our Web site, you can access the selections on the CD-ROM by clicking the "Preview" button for a particular selection. The CD-ROM will automatically launch the reading you have selected.

MINIMUM SYSTEM REQUIREMENTS:

Windows Users

- i486 or Pentium processor-based personal computer
- Microsoft Windows 95, Windows 98, or Windows NT 4.0 with Service pack 3 or later
- 10 MB of available RAM on Windows 95 and Windows 98 (16 MB recommended)
- 16 MB of available RAM on Windows NT (24 recommended)
- Acrobat Reader 4.0 (included on this CD-ROM)
- 10 MB of available hard-disk space

Mac Users

- Apple Macintosh or compatible computer
- Mac OS software version 7.1.2 or later
- 4.5 MB of available RAM (6.5 MB recommended)
- Acrobat Reader 4.0 (included on this CD-ROM; requires Power PC for installation)
- 8 MB of available hard-disk space

3. **Build your custom reader** Follow the easy, step-by-step instructions on our Web site to build your book online. It's as simple as registering, choosing your selections, and submitting your request.

4. **Placing your order with your bookstore** Within two days of receiving your custom reader request, a custom publishing representative will contact you with a price confirmation and all the details you will need to complete your order. Once these elements have been confirmed, you will receive an ISBN, which you will need to submit directly to your bookstore. Your bookstore must then send a purchase order to our custom publishing manager to order printing.

Please direct inquiries to:

Jane Smith
Custom Publishing Manager
Bedford/St. Martin's
33 Irving Place
New York, NY 10003
Fax: 212-253-1385
Phone: 212-375-7105
E-mail: customreader@bedfordstmartins.com
URL: http://customreader.bedfordstmartins.com

ORDERING/PRICING INFORMATION FOR *THE ST. MARTIN'S CUSTOM READER*

Minimum Order

The minimum initial order is 100 copies; the minimum reorder is 10 copies. However, within unit adoptions of 500 copies or more, there is some opportunity for customization for individual instructors.

Pricing

The St. Martin's Custom Reader has a base price of $5, plus an additional charge of $.10 per page. There will be an additional charge of $.35 per page for the inclusion of extra, outside material (for example, a syllabus, course materials, or research guidelines from your school library). The minimum price for any custom reader is $10 net. (Net price is the price to your bookstore, and subject to the bookstore's additional markup.) Once you've built your book, you will be contacted by a custom publishing representative to confirm price.

Production Time

It will take anywhere from 6 to 8 weeks for delivery on an initial order. Reorders will take 1 to 2 weeks for delivery. Note that production time begins only when Bedford/St. Martin's receives the order from your bookstore.

Ordering

To order *The St. Martin's Custom Reader*, go to our Web site at http://customreader.bedfordstmartins.com. Follow the easy, step-by-step instructions to build your book online. Alternatively, you can fax us a printed order form, available on the CD-ROM included at the back of this booklet.

Within two days of receiving your custom reader request, a custom publishing representative will contact you to confirm price and to issue an ISBN, which you will need to submit directly to your bookstore. Your bookstore must then send to our custom publishing manager a purchase order that contains the bookstore name, phone number, textbook manager's name, the ISBN of your custom reader, and the total number of books you'll need for your class. Before we can begin printing your custom reader, we must have that purchase order, so you might want to confirm with your bookstore that the purchase order has been sent.

Additional Material

You can incorporate additional materials into your custom reader—for example, a syllabus, course materials, or research guidelines from your school library. These additional materials will appear at the end of your custom reader, following the selections you have chosen from the database. Please note that the material will need to be submitted to Bedford/St. Martin's as camera-ready copy and that its inclusion will add 1 to 2 weeks to your production time. For details on how to include your own material in your custom reader, contact our Custom Publishing Department (e-mail: customreader@bedfordstmartins.com) or ask the custom publishing representative about this option when you are confirming the details of your order.

Discount Packages

You can package *The St. Martin's Custom Reader* with any Bedford/St. Martin's titles at a discounted price. If you package with one or more of our titles, we'll discount the total price by 10 percent. Please note that packages will add 2 weeks to your production time.

Customized Cover

To ensure that each student purchases the correct version of *The St. Martin's Custom Reader*, each cover is printed with the instructor's name and course information. Once you've created a table of contents, you will need to submit this information to us on the "Create Cover" page of our Web site. You can also preview your cover on this page.

Desk Copies

Please order desk copies from the custom publishing representative when you submit your initial custom reader request.